Advanced Soap Making: Removing the Mystery

Mary Humphrey
Alyssa Middleton

Advanced Soap Making: Removing the Mystery
By Mary Humphrey and Alyssa Middleton

Editing by Crowdsourced Team: Elin Criswell, Shila Laing, Teri Patterson, Alana Rivera, Anne Marie Rowe, Robin Schmidt, Maia Singletary, Rachel Turner, and Ann Wooledge

ISBN-13: 978-0615894843 (Beauty For Ashes Press)
ISBN-10: 0615894844

Notice of Rights

Notice of Liability

Disclaimer

DEDICATION

This book is dedicated to you, the creative person that purchased this book! We hope your soap making endeavors last a lifetime, accompanied with great joy while capturing and fulfilling your dreams and God-given talents.

TABLE OF CONTENTS

ACKNOWLEDGMENTS

Mary's acknowledgements:

As I start each day, and as I write each word, it is with infinite gratefulness to the one that provides for me and holds my pen, Jesus Christ. I love you so very much.

On this earth, I dedicate my life to you, Bob, the beautiful man that loves and believes in me, for better and for worse. You help to make my life complete. With your never ending support, I have the God-given freedom to develop and complete my mission in life.

I give special thanks to my sister, Georgia, an unfailing companion. You've given so much of you to me, even at times when the sacrifice was large. I am blessed to have a sister such as you, one that unselfishly gives friendship and love.

Alyssa's acknowledgements:

All the glory and praise to my Lord and Savior, Jesus Christ. There can never be enough praise from my lips to thank You for saving me and blessing me as You do. May everything I do bring You glory and honor.

To AWM & both of my precious AMM's: Je t'aimerai toujours!

A special thanks to my co-author and friend, Mary: it has been a blessing and honor writing two books with you. I am so thankful we took this leap of faith together, and I hope we have the opportunity to work together again!

INTRODUCTION

Welcome to *Advanced Soap Making: Removing the Mystery!*

Between the covers of this book you will find a complete and detailed volume of cold process soap making methods focused on beneficial and alternative soap making ingredients. You will no longer be confused and challenged while spending hours on end thumbing from book to book, or internet site to site. Instead, this book contains all that you need.

Have you ever wanted to master goat milk soap? We've made it more than easy with detailed instructions and tips. Have you considered including non-traditional liquids, such as wine or beer? We've broken those down for you as well.

There is so much to learn about soap making, with many unique and common ingredients to choose from. What a joy! In addition to teaching alternative techniques, we've helped you out by covering:

- Colorants
- Clays
- Fruit and vegetable purees
- Hardeners
- Herbs
- Natural scent blending

Confused by soap making terminology? We have an extensive glossary for your reference.

What about your soap making troubles? Don't let them get you down. We have you covered with our troubleshooting section, where we share mistakes we've made over the years and how you can avoid these same mistakes in your soaps.

You want to know how to scent your soap with essential oils? It is all in our details: essential oil list, INCI names, description, properties, safe usage, along with a bonus to round out your knowledge – a section on scent blending. If you haven't already done so, you will want to make your own blends. As a soap maker, you will be eager to take fragrance one step further and make your soap uniquely yours!

Our years of successful soap making experience have been combined in this book. Mary Humphrey of Annie's Goat Hill Handcrafted Soaps has ten years of soap making and four years of aromatherapy experience. Alyssa Middleton of Vintage Body Spa and Bath and Body Academy has eight years of soap making experience and has also extensively studied aromatherapy and herbs in creating her own formulas. This results in a unique and thorough compilation of soap making tips and instructions.

We've published this book to help you flourish as a soap maker and to lead you to even greater inspiration. We want to help <u>you</u> become a master soap maker, so turn the page and let's begin!

CHAPTER 1
SOAP MAKING REFRESHER

We know that most of you purchased this book with some cold process soap making experience and are now ready to read about more advanced soap making methods. However, the bridging of basic soap making with uncommon ingredients and advanced techniques is successful only if the basic techniques that a soap maker follows are sound. For this reason, we have started this book with our simple refresher course in soap making, safety and instructions.

"After several years of soap making I learned to study and treasure even the most basic of soap making instructions, especially words from other experienced soap makers. This often steered me to a renewed understanding, and sometimes it resulted in uncovering unsuccessful habits that I had developed." - Mary

Soap Making 101

What is soap?
The combination of an acid (oils) and a base (alkaline, specifically lye) forms a neutral salt, commonly known as soap. The chemical process that causes the oils and alkaline to make soap is called saponification (oils + alkaline = soap).

Soap is a surfactant that works in two ways: it first helps water to disperse on the skin instead of pooling into droplets, and then propels dirt and oil away from the skin. Water does not mix with oil, soap lifts the dirt and oil from the skin through lather.

Detergents are also considered surfactants. The value of handmade soap is that it is gentle, unlike detergents. Handmade soap naturally contains beneficial ingredients, such as glycerin, that help the skin retain moisture.

How is soap made?

The four main methods in handcrafted soap making are:

Cold Process – Oils are heated and then cooled to a certain temperature. A lye/liquid mixture is added to the oils to create a reaction called saponification. Soap is formed within 24 hours, and is cured (becomes mild and hardened) within 4-6 weeks. This is the method we focus on in this book.

Hot Process – Oils are mixed with a lye/liquid mixture and are cooked using a slow heat method. This method is often used to reduce the soap's cure time. We do not advise inexperienced soap makers to use this method. Hot process soap making can produce a bar of soap that is less smooth in texture, and is difficult to incorporate certain ingredients, such as milk.

Melt-and-Pour - A premade soap base is melted and poured into molds. The soap maker can add a range of ingredients, including colorants, fragrance and some additional oils to the melted soap base. Making this type of soap can save soap making time as the soap hardens and can be used within hours. Many melt and pour soap bases contain surfactants that are considered detergents.

Milled (often called French or hand milled) - Pre-made hot process or cold process soap is grated, mixed with liquids, gently heated and pressed into molds. Additional ingredients can also be added to the soap, such as fragrance and some oils. Because the additional ingredients do not go through a heat process, benefits to this type of soap are scent that does not fade, and oils or butters that hold their moisturizing properties.

Ingredients Used in Soap Making

Liquids

Water is the most common liquid used in soap making. As this book focuses on advanced soap making techniques, we discuss alternative liquids that can also be used including milk, beer, wine, tea and coffee along with the specific steps necessary to safely and effectively incorporate these liquids into your formula.

We recommend using distilled water in your formulas, which is inexpensive and easily found at the grocery store. Distilled water is more stable to use than regular tap water because the impurities have been removed.

Oils

Any number or combination of oils can be used when making soap, and each oil reacts differently with lye to create unique properties in soap. In Chapter 3 we discuss different properties and benefits of specific oils and butters when used in soap making. Learning what each ingredient's benefits include will help in creating unique formulas based on your specific needs.

There are two types of oils: soft and hard. Soft oils like olive or sunflower are those that are liquid at room temperature. Soft oils contribute to the conditioning factor of the finished soap. Hard oils such as coconut or palm are those that are solid at room temperature. Hard oils help to make a bar of soap hard after it has cured, and most will find that soap made with hard oils tend to last longer than soap made with only soft oils. The exception to this is Castile soap, which is soap made from only olive oil. Although Castile soap takes a long time to fully cure (12 weeks or more), the end result is a nice, hard bar of soap.

Most soap is hard enough to unmold within 24-48 hours. Using a high percentage of soft oils in a formula may lengthen that time.

Most soap formulas use a combination of soft and hard oils, many with a ratio of 60 percent hard oils to 40 percent soft oils. Select your own combination of oils to create a bar of soap with the hardness, conditioning, lathering and cleaning properties you prefer.

"Speaking of soap ingredients, if you have available space and if you intend to make numerous batches of soap, you might consider storing your ingredients pre-measured.

I measure hard oils into plastic containers with tight fitting lids, along with separate containers for soft oils. I also pre-measure lye (stored in small very tight containers with screw on lids - see lye caution statements on pages 17-18).

I use a different color lid for each ingredient type.

Between the organization of the oils and the pre-measurements, I save time, which allows me to make soap whenever I need without digging through the larger containers of oils and butters.

Pre-measuring also saves on clean up. If you've already pre-measured olive oil, for example, you can use the same container several times without having to wash it over and over again." - Mary

Soap Making Equipment/Products Needed

Another great thing about soap making is that it does not require a lot of expensive or difficult to find tools and equipment. Once you have used a piece of equipment for soap making, it should be kept separate from other kitchen utensils and not used for preparing food. The equipment should <u>only</u> be used for soap making.

Because lye reacts with most metals, use glass, enamel, plastic or stainless steel utensils and mixing containers. Do not use disposable materials such as Styrofoam or paper.

Besides safety equipment (goggles, rubber gloves and apron), a scale is one of the most important pieces of equipment in soap making. Incorrect measurements will lead to a failed batch of soap. Each ingredient reacts with the lye solution at a specific rate, so precise measurement is critical to ensure that saponification occurs. Purchase an electronic digital scale that measures in tenths of ounces, grams, and also has the tare function.

Additional equipment needed for soap making:

- Workspace covering such as newspaper, cardboard or a vinyl tablecloth. This protects your counters from any stray droplets of lye water or fresh soap that may accidentally spill.

- Lye-resistant container for measuring sodium hydroxide. Stainless steel, glass or heat-resistant plastic are the best materials for these containers.

- Large, heat-resistant container for measuring water and mixing lye solution and for pouring the lye solution into the oils. These include: heavy glass (high heat and caustic materials can lead to the shattering of thin glass), stainless steel (aluminum discolors and can causing the leaching of metal that affects the end product), and heavy plastics (thin plastics may melt or etch from caustic materials and heat).

- Measuring cups and spoons made of plastic or stainless steel.

- A soap pot in which to mix the lye solution and oils. Some use a slow cooker for this purpose. Large stainless steel soup pots also work well.

- Spoons - Choose stainless steel or heavy plastic. Do not use wooden spoons, as they can splinter from the high temperatures of lye water and/or soap mixture.

- Thermometers - These will help you determine the temperature of your lye mixture and oils before mixing. Do not use a glass thermometer, as it can fracture or chip. Do use a thermometer that can be inserted into the mixture or ingredients, such as a metal meat thermometer, or a digital thermometer with a probe. Laser thermometers tend to read surface temperature only., so we do not recommend using them for soap making.

- Spatula - These can be silicone or heavy duty rubber.

- Soap molds - These can be wooden, acrylic or silicone. A one to five pound capacity mold is suitable for most soap makers.

- Stick blender - A basic model with a low speed setting is sufficient and will save you untold time in bringing your soap mixture to trace as compared to stirring by hand.

- Blankets or heavy towels for insulating the filled soap molds.

- Cutter/blade to cut the soap loaf into separate bars - these can be straight or wavy, depending on the type of finish you'd like on your soap - smooth or with ridges.

- Cooling racks on which the soap bars will cure until ready to use.

"Soap making equipment and utensils do not have to win beauty contests, nor do they need to be an expensive, top of the line purchase. Stackable stainless steel lightweight pots purchased at a discount store meet the task at hand just as well as heavy expensive pots from a specialty store. You can also reuse plastic gallon (and larger) sized containers that oils are shipped in as free mixing pots.

A brand new stainless steel shelving system works well as a cooling rack for curing soap, but so do old (clean) oven and refrigerator racks. The name of the cost saving game is to be creative-put your money into soap making ingredients and not expensive equipment, fixtures and utensils.

Yard sales and restaurants (items that are old and being tossed out) are great places to find functional equipment, fixtures and utensils. If you want to spend money on stainless steel tables or commercial equipment, an auction is a great starting place. I once purchased an entire room full of tables and cabinets at a fraction of the cost compared to used equipment at the restaurant supply house.

I do recommend investing in a decent stick blender. Lower cost stick blenders work well for a short period of time. If you do purchase one that is less expensive my recommendation is to have several on hand just in case a motor burns out in the middle of mixing soap." - Mary

Before You Start Soap Making

Be sure to use clean, dry equipment and utensils. Be sure to follow Good Manufacturing Practices (GMP), which include among other things, sterilization and proper workplace preparation. At this time, GMP is recommended, not required by the United States government for soap makers, but is a requirement for cosmetic manufacturers. There are variances in regulations, so check with your local municipality. For more information on Good Manufacturing Practices, visit the FDA's website: www.fda.govCosmeticsGuidanceComplianceRegulatoryInformation/ GoodManufacturingPracticeGMPGuidelinesInspectionChecklist/ default.htm.

The formulas in this book are by weight, not volume. To make sure measurements are accurate, you must tare or zero out the scale *before* preparing to measure out your ingredients. To do this, follow these steps:

1. Place the empty container in which you plan to measure the ingredient (i.e., a bowl), on the scale.

2. Press "on" or "tare." The scale will set to zero.

3. Put the ingredient into the bowl and the scale will only measure the weight of the ingredient, not the weight of the bowl.

Safety First - Using Sodium Hydroxide (Lye)

Sodium hydroxide (NaOH) is also known as lye or caustic soda. It is necessary for saponification, the chemical process by which oils and lye combine and form bar soap. Without lye, there is no soap. Be sure not to confuse sodium hydroxide with potassium hydroxide (KOH), which is used to make liquid soap.

Always purchase sodium hydroxide (NaOH) from reputable suppliers. Do not use sodium yydroxide products, commonly known as drain cleaners that can be found at hardware stores. These products contain small amounts of dangerous ingredients that are not safe for soap making. Ensure the sodium hydroxide that you buy is labeled 100% pure, not 99.9% or any other percentage.

Handle sodium hydroxide and a lye solution (the solution made when lye is mixed with a liquid - water, goat milk, etc.) with care. Sodium hydroxide crystals and lye solutions are very caustic and can easily cause chemical burns.

Tips

Store lye in a sealed, unbreakable container, and well out of the reach of children and pets. The package should be clearly labeled with the proper warnings: Poison, Harmful if swallowed, Keep out of reach of children, etc.

Never handle lye without wearing the proper safety equipment: safety goggles (lye will cause blindness if it gets into the eyes), gloves, mask, long sleeves, pants and closed-toed shoes. To avoid the possibility of a chemical burn if any lye splashes on you, you want to have as much of your skin covered as possible.

Only start the soap making process when you have a large chunk of uninterrupted time. You will need to focus on the task at hand and cannot be interrupted or you will risk making a serious and potentially harmful mistake. As an additional safety measure before you start the process, organize all of your materials and equipment in a manner that will avoid accidents, such as tripping, or spills. Avoid using caustic materials, such as lye, when children are present.

Only open the lye container immediately before measuring it for your formula. As soon as you are done measuring, close the container.

Work in a well-ventilated area when mixing lye. Lye emits strong vapors. When creating a lye solution, do not stand directly over the mixing container to avoid inhaling the vapors. Wearing a properly fitted facemask that protects the nasal passages and membranes will ensure you do not inhale fumes. There are various types of protective masks available, from thin cloth or paper that provide a very low level of protection, to those that contain vapor cartridges that offer a very high degree of protection.

To prevent splashing of the caustic mixture onto your skin, and to prevent the bubbling up of the mixture, always add lye to your liquid (water, goat milk, etc.). An often-repeated phrase in the soaping world is, "It always snows on water." This helps you remember to pour the white lye flakes into the liquid, rather than the other way around.

Lye solution is extremely hot due to the chemical reaction involved. Use caution when handling the lye solution mixing container.

Should you come into contact with lye, immediately rinse your skin with vinegar. Vinegar is an acid and it will help balance out the high alkaline level of the lye, which will slow or stop the burning. Then rinse with water.

Disposing of Lye

Lye is considered a hazardous substance and therefore has specific instructions and considerations as to how it can be disposed. As hazardous waste, lye is subject to federal, state and local disposal regulations. Be sure to check with your local hazardous waste collection agency to find out the specific disposal instructions for your area.

Do **not** pour lye down your sink drain, into a toilet, on the ground or into the trash. Lye cannot be thrown out with your everyday trash.

Most soap makers use all of their lye in the soap making process, however, spills may occur, necessitating disposal of contaminated lye. Do **not** dispose of lye in a plastic or aluminum container, since lye can corrode through the plastic or aluminum. Be sure to clearly mark the disposal container with poison warnings and symbols.

Never reuse your lye containers for any other purpose.

Now that we have discussed safety precautions and disposal of lye, let's move on to preparing soap molds and soap making steps.

Wooden Mold Preparation

1. Using freezer paper with a plastic coating, line the wooden mold, using one piece for the center and bottom section, and one piece each for the two ends. Always line the mold with the plastic coated side up.

2. For the ends of the mold, cut lining pieces to fit and place in each end of the mold. Using your fingers, crease the paper at the bottom of the mold, about ½" from the paper edge. Fold excess paper over the top of the mold.

3. For the sides of the mold, cut pieces to fit and place the lining. Use your fingers to crease the paper at the bottom of the mold. Fold any excess paper over the top of the mold. Smooth out any wrinkles prior to pouring the soap mixture into the mold. Wrinkles in the paper will leave small indentations in the finished soap.

Note: No preparation is needed for silicone molds. Read the manufacturer's guidelines before using the mold.

Soap Making Steps

1. Put on all of your safety gear: goggles, mask and heavy-duty gloves.

2. Weigh your lye in a glass or heavy plastic container. Set container aside.

3. Measure distilled water and pour into a glass or heavy plastic pitcher or other container with a pouring spout. Remember to use distilled water.

4. **Slowly** pour the measured lye into the water. Stir until all the lye crystals dissolve. The mixture will become cloudy, but keep stirring until the lye is completely dissolved and the mixture becomes clear. Avoid inhaling the emitted fumes during this process. The mixture will also heat up, so avoid touching the mixing container without any protection. Set the lye solution aside to cool while you are mixing the other ingredients.

5. Measure out the remaining ingredients needed for your formula, including fragrances and additives. Measuring everything out in the beginning saves you from overlooking an ingredient, and helps ensure your soap making process will be smooth.

6. Now it is time to melt the oils. First melt the hard oils over low heat. You may be tempted to melt everything on high to speed up the process, but this may scorch the oils. You need to wait for the lye to significantly cool down, so there is no need to rush this part of the process.

Safety Note: Oils can catch fire when they are overheated. Always stay next to your melting pot and monitor the temperature while heating oils.

7. Once your hard oils are melted, add the liquid oils. Stir gently with your spoon.

8. Remove from heat (or if using a slow cooker, turn it off and remove the crock from the heating source) and measure the temperature of the oil mixture with a thermometer.

9. With another thermometer, measure the temperature of the lye. Ideally, the temperature for both the lye solution and the melted oils will be 100°F. This is a good temperature to start with when making soap. Over time, you may decide to use a different temperature, but for initial batches, stick with 100°F as a rule of thumb.

If either or both the lye solution or the oils are too hot, then place the containers into a sink with ice water. Be sure not to put too much ice water into the sink or it will make the containers float and spill over.

If the oils are too cold, simply return the container to the stovetop or slow cooker and heat until they've reached approximately 100°F.

10. Slowly pour your lye solution into the melted oils and stir with a spoon or soap stirrer until you have a uniformly colored mixture.

11. Start mixing with your stick blender.

12. As you feel and see the mixture getting thicker, test the mixture for "trace." Trace is when you turn off the stick blender, lift it out of the mixture and let the soap on the blender head dribble into the mixture below. If the drops sit on top of the mixture for a moment before sinking in, you have reached trace. This may be a fast process or it could take a while, depending on the oils used in your formula. Stop mixing at this point. You do not want to have thick trace (where the mixture looks like pudding), as this may make it difficult to add in fragrance and/or additives.

13. Add in any additives and superfatting oil(s). Stir slightly with the stick blender to disperse the additives throughout the mixture.

14. Add in the fragrance or essential oils and mix with the stick blender until everything is combined well.

15. Your soap will be at thick trace now, almost a pudding consistency and is now ready to be poured. Pour into your prepared mold.

16. When all the soap has been poured into the mold, put the lid on top of the soap (or cover with plastic wrap if a lid is not available).

17. Wrap the mold in towels or small blankets to keep the temperature of the soap from cooling too quickly, or soda ash can form. Soda ash is a thin layer of white ash that forms on the top of soap. It can be cut off, but it is much easier to avoid soda ash in the first place. Keep the soap insulated for about 24 hours. Resist the temptation to peek in on your soap. If you do, the trapped heat needed to continue the curing process will be released.

After the soap is poured into the mold, covered and wrapped, it might go into the gel phase. During the gel phase the temperature of the soap increases and the soap becomes translucent and gel-like in appearance. The gel phase allows the soap to fully saponify, which chemically changes the fats, oils, and caustic materials to soap.

18. After about 24 hours, your soap will be firm in the mold. Carefully remove the soap log from the mold. If you have difficulties in releasing your soap, it may need more time in the mold. Let it sit for another 12-24 hours. If after that time you still cannot get the soap out of the mold, then refer to the mold manufacturer's website to see what they recommend for their particular mold(s); it may be putting the mold into the oven on a low temperature, or some manufacturers will recommend putting their mold(s) into the freezer. Follow manufacturer's directions so you don't damage the mold.

19. Cut your soap into bars using a cutter or blade.

20. Place the cut bars onto a rack to cure. Let the soap cure for 4-6 weeks so that the rest of the water can evaporate and the soap can become even harder and milder. Every few days flip the bars in a different direction, on each side, to one end, then the other, so that each side of the bar is exposed to air during the curing process.

21. Voila! Your soaps are ready!

Cleaning Tips

Once you have finished making soap, clean the area as soon as possible to avoid the challenge of washing hardened soap off of surfaces and utensils.

Always wear gloves while cleaning to avoid burns from contact with caustic (unsaponified) soap.

As soon as you are finished with the stick blender, **unplug the unit** and detach the mixing wand. Carefully wipe the blade area with paper towels to remove excess soap. Set the wand, upright and blade side down, in a container of hot sudsy water. This will help to soften and remove soap from hard to reach places around the blades.

Scrape excess soap from the mixing pot and use paper towels to wipe any additional soap from the interior, lip or exterior of the pot. If there is too much soap for a paper towel to hold, scrape the soap into a throw away container, or onto several thicknesses of newspaper and roll up. Fill the pot with hot sudsy water to soak. Wipe excess soap from any remaining utensils and containers and place them in the sudsy water in the mixing pot, or the sink, to soak.

A concentrated dish soap made especially for grease cutting works well for soaking and washing soap utensils.

Using paper, such as newspaper, to cover the work table while soap making helps to protect work surfaces and eases the cleanup process. Once soap making is finished, all you need to do is roll up the newspaper and throw it away.

Keep a trash container with a heavy bag liner close by while completing clean up. You will be tossing in the paper towels, newspapers, and other materials that contain remnants of caustic soap.

Wiping the utensils and soap pot with paper towels before soaking and washing eliminates excess raw soap from entering the plumbing drains, and helps to keep the wash water grease free and less caustic.

"Many soap makers use a high percentage vinegar (and water) spray or rinse on their soap utensils and pots, and some add vinegar to their soak water to help break down oil and caustic soap remnants. The use of vinegar is a personal choice, it has not been proven scientifically as an agent that reduces the caustic properties of lye or soap. I personally have used vinegar successfully on lye burns caused by contact with raw soap on my skin." - Mary

CHAPTER 2
ALTERNATIVE SOAP MAKING METHODS

In this chapter we'll discuss three alternative methods to making soap: Room Temperature Cold Process, Thermal Transfer and Water Discounting. Each are considered advanced techniques because they require previous soap making experience.

Room Temperature Cold Process

Room Temperature Cold Process, or RTCP is a method in which you mix your oils and lye when both are at room temperature. This method allows the soap maker to premix the oils and lye solution in advance and store them in separate containers in a safe location until it is time to completely mix all of the ingredients to make soap. RTCP can also save time because there is no need to wait for the lye solution to cool nor to warm the oils to the same temperature as the lye solution.

There are no additional preparation steps or equipment needed to use RTCP. Rather, you use fewer pieces of equipment, since there are no ice baths to cool the lye solution and no thermometers needed.

Making RTCP soap is a fairly easy process. Simply follow these steps after preparing your soap molds and measuring out the ingredients including any additives or scent.

Steps

1. Measure out and melt the solid oils and place into your soaping container.

2. Measure your liquid oils and add to the soaping container.

3. Use your stick blender to mix the oils well and set the soaping container aside.

4. Prepare your lye solution, using standard soap making procedures and following all safety precautions. Set lye solution aside to cool. Once cooled, place a lid over the container and store safely in a secure location, away from children and pets.

5. When you are ready to make soap, follow standard soap making procedures.

Thermal Transfer Cold Process

Thermal Transfer Cold Process, or TTCP is a method in which the heat from the lye solution is used to melt the solid oils into liquid. This method is used to save time. There is no need to wait for both the lye solution to cool to the recommended temperature nor to warm the oils to the identical temperature. There are some things to note, however about TTCP:

- The ingredients in your formula will determine whether or not TTCP will work for you. If you have a high amount of solid oils such as cocoa butter, shea butter, beeswax, coconut, etc (especially those with higher melting points) the heat from the lye solution may not be strong enough to melt the oils. You may need to cut the solid oils into small pieces to facilitate melting, or pop them in the microwave to soften/start the melting process.

- The temperature of your soaping area can greatly affect the likelihood of TTCP being successful. It will take more heat to melt oils that are in a cold room. If your workspace is in a cool room you may need to melt the solid oils in your formula in advance.

Steps

1. Measure the solid and liquid oils and place into your soaping container.

2. Use a stick blender to create a slurry.

3. Prepare your lye solution, using standard soap making procedures and following all safety precautions.

4. Slowly pour the lye solution over the oil slurry in the soaping pot.

5. Gently stir the lye solution/solid oils with a wire whisk, submerging the chunks of solid oils into the solution to aid in the melting process. Continue until all solid oils have melted. This may take a few minutes.

6. Continue with standard soap making procedures.

Water Discounting

Another alternative method to making soap is called Water Discount. This means the amount of water used in the formula is discounted, or reduced.

Soap makers use a water discount to reduce waste (since the water simply evaporates from the finished bar of soap over time), or to shorten the drying time as the less water that needs to evaporate from the finished bar of soap creates a harder bar of soap in a shorter amount of time.

Should you decide to use a water discount, be extra cautious with the lye solution as it will be even stronger since there is more lye in the solution and less water, so it will be even more caustic.

Also note that when using a water discount, your formula may trace faster, and you may run into problems including seizing and ricing. Therefore, only decrease the water amount in your formula by a slight amount each time and take detailed notes so that you can determine the effects that a water discount has on your formula. For instance, if your formula calls for 6 ounces of water, drop that down to 5.5 ounces and take notes on how the soap mixture reacts, how quickly the soap hardens, etc. Next time you make that formula, you can opt to decrease the water just a little bit more. It is not recommended to use more than a 50 percent water discount.

It is often easiest to calculate a water discount using a lye calculator, which we discuss in more detail in Chapter 14. Here is an example of what the same formula looks like using a water discount, using the lye calculator from SoapCalc. Note that the standard setting in SoapCalc for water is 38% of the oil weight in the formula.

Castile Soap Formula (Non-Water Discount)
Pomace olive oil	16 ounces
Sodium hydroxide	2.04 ounces
Distilled water	6.08 ounces

Castile Soap Formula (Water Discount to 35% of oil weight)
Pomace olive oil	16 ounces
Sodium hydroxide	2.04 ounces
Distilled water	5.60 ounces

Castile Soap Formula (Water Discount to 30% of oil weight)
Pomace olive oil	16 ounces
Sodium hydroxide	2.04 ounces
Distilled water	4.80 ounces

You'll notice that many of our formulas in this book use a water discount. As we've gained experience over the years, we've incorporated water discounts into all of our formulas. You'll read later in the book about instances in which you should **not** use water discounts, as taking a water discount with certain ingredients can cause your batch of soap to fail-lessons we learned the hard way!

"I tend to use Thermal Transfer when soaping. It makes the process go a little bit faster and is easier not having to worry about exact temperatures. It's also a more eco-friendly method of soaping, since it uses no electricity. I have never run into any issues when making soap with this process." - Alyssa

CHAPTER 3
OILS, BUTTERS AND SUPERFATTING

Next we'll discuss a variety of soap making oils and butters. Many new soap makers tend to stick with the 'Holy Trinity' of oils: coconut, olive and palm. This chapter discusses other oils and butters - some common and some quite exotic - that can be incorporated into your formulas. If you've ever wondered 'How would XYZ oil react in soap?,' here's where you'll learn that information!

Following the ingredient name, we've listed a number of items that will help you as you create your own formulas:

- *International Nomenclature of Cosmetic Ingredients* (INCI) Provides listings of the proper ingredients' name for soap labeling.

- Saponification (SAP) value of each so that you know the amount of milligrams of sodium hydroxide that is required to saponify 1 gram of oil or butter. This information is necessary if you are going to manually calculate your formulas as we discuss in Chapter 14.

- Melt point describes the temperature at which the butter melts and becomes liquefied.

- Fatty Acids explain the type and concentration of fatty acids that each ingredient contains. The table on the next page explains the qualities that each type of fatty acid brings to your soap.

- Shelf Life is the length of time the oil is stable for soap making before it may start to go rancid. Shelf life is highly dependent upon how the oil is stored, though. For best results, store oils in a cool, dry location. We've listed the average shelf life in our descriptions. Actual shelf life may vary by supplier and manufacturer.

- Description of the ingredients' properties and benefits.

General Qualities that Some Fatty Acids Bring to Soap

	Hard	Cleansing	Conditioning	Bubbly Lather	Creamy Lather
Lauric	X	X		X	
Linoleic			X		
Linolenic			X		
Myristic	X	X		X	
Oleic			X		
Palmitic	X				X
Ricinoleic			X	X	X
Stearic	X				X

Hard (Solid) Oils/Butters:

Babassu Oil
INCI: *Orbignya oleifera*
Label Name: Orbignya oleifera (Babassu) Seed Oil
SAP Value: .175
Melt Point: 75° F
Fatty Acids:50% Lauric, 20% Myristic, 11% Palmitic, 10% Oleic, 4% Stearic
Shelf Life: 1 year
Babassu oil is pressed from the nuts of the Babassu palm tree found primarily in Brazil. Solid at room temperature, this whitish butter melts upon skin contact. It has properties similar to coconut oil. In soap, babassu contributes to a hard soap with thick, bubbly lather. It may speed up trace. Use up to 25% of your formula. DO NOT USE IF YOU HAVE NUT ALLERGIES.

Beeswax
INCI: *Cera alba*
Label Name: Cera alba (Beeswax)
SAP Value: .067
Melt Point: 145° F
Fatty Acids: Does not contain fatty acids
Shelf Life: stable
Though not an oil, beeswax can be saponified, so we have included it in this section. Unrefined beeswax is yellow and has a honey scent, which may be slightly noticeable in finished soap. Beeswax can be used to harden a bar of soap, and may also protect against the light layer of ash that can form on finished soap. Use at less than 2% of your total formula. More can create a sticky bar of soap with decreased lather that drags across the skin.

Cocoa Butter

INCI: *Theobroma cacao*
Label Name: Theobroma cacao (Cocoa) Seed Butter
SAP Value: .136
Melt Point: 96° F
Fatty Acids: 35% Oleic, 33% Stearic, 28% Palmitic, 3% Linoleic
Shelf Life: 2 years

Cocoa butter is a pale-yellow, edible vegetable fat extracted from the cocoa bean. It is solid at room temperature, but melts upon skin contact. In soap, cocoa butter creates a hard, conditioning bar with a stable lather. It may also lead to a quicker trace. Using too much cocoa butter can make your soap bars brittle or crack while curing. Therefore, keep this butter at less than 15% in your formula or use it (melted) as a superfatting oil.

Coconut Oil

INCI: *Cocos nucifera*
Label Name: Cocos nucifera (Coconut) Oil
SAP Value: .180
Melt Point: 76° F or 92° F, depending on the type of coconut oil used
Fatty Acids: 48% Lauric, 19% Myristic, 9% Palmitic, 8% Oleic, 3% Stearic, 2% Linoleic
Shelf Life: 2 years

Coconut oil is refined from the meat of the coconut. It is a yellowish white oil that is solid at room temperature (under 76°), but liquefies at higher temperatures and melts upon skin contact. Coconut oil has a very long shelf life. In soap, coconut oil creates a hard, white bar of soap with fluffy lather. Coconut oil can also increase trace. Too much coconut oil can be drying to the skin, so be sure to use no more than 30% in your formula.

Cupuacu Butter

INCI: *Theobroma grandiflorum*
Label Name: Theobroma grandiflorum (Cupuacu) Butter
SAP Value: .136
Melt Point: 94° F
Fatty Acids: 44% Oleic, 31% Stearic, 7% Palmitic, 5% Linoleic
Shelf Life: 2 years

Cupuacu Butter is extracted by cold pressing the seeds of the Cupuacu tree, which is native to the Amazon rainforest. It is hard at room temperature and has a very thick and creamy consistency. Cupuacu butter also has a mild and sweet aroma that is not noticeable in finished soap. It contributes to a hard, conditioning bar with stable lather. Use up to 15% of your formula, or as a superfatting agent.

Illipe Butter
INCI: *Shorea stenoptera*
Label Name: Shorea stenoptera (Illipe) Seed Butter
SAP Value: .132
Melt Point: 91° F
Fatty Acids: 45% Stearic, 35% Oleic, 17% Palmitic
Shelf Life: 2 years
Illipe Butter is pressed from the nuts of the Shorea tree, which is native to Southeast Asia. It is a hard, creamy white butter with very little scent. Illipe is similar in composition to cocoa butter, and is sometimes used in soap making as a cocoa butter substitute. In soap, it contributes to a hard, cleansing bar with stable lather. Use up to 15% of your formula, or as a superfatting agent. DO NOT USE IF YOU HAVE NUT ALLERGIES.

Kokum Butter
INCI: *Garcinia indica*
Label Name: Garcinia indica (Kokum) Seed Butter
SAP Value: .135
Melt Point: 102° F
Fatty Acids: 56% Stearic, 36% Oleic, 4% Palmitic, 1% Linoleic
Shelf Life: 2 years
Kokum Butter comes from the fruit kernel of the Garcinia Indica tree, which is native to India. It is a very hard, yellowish white butter with an earthy scent that is not noticeable in finished soap. Kokum butter can be used as a substitute for cocoa butter, as it is similar in hardness and emollient properties. It contributes to a hard bar of soap with stable lather. Use up to 15% of your formula, or as a superfatting agent.

Lard
INCI: Lard
Label Name: Lard
SAP Value: .138
Melt Point: 95° F
Fatty Acids: 46% Oleic, 28% Palmitic, 13% Stearic, 6% Linoleic, 1% Myristic
Shelf Life: 4-6 months
Lard is an inexpensive, semisolid fat that comes from pigs and is used as an economical base for soap making. Lard creates a very hard, white bar of soap that has a light creamy, stable lather. Use up to 50-70% of your formula to prevent finished soap from becoming brittle. Lard may speed up trace. Lard can go rancid within 4-6 months, but the shelf life may be extended to 6-12 months if kept refrigerated in a tightly closed container.

Mango Butter

INCI: *Mangifera indica*

Label Name: Mangifera indica (Mango) Seed Butter

SAP Value: .134

Melt Point: 100° F

Fatty Acids: 45% Oleic, 42% Stearic, 7% Palmitic, 3% Linoleic

Shelf Life: 1 year

Mango butter is obtained from the kernels of the Mango tree. It is a yellowish white butter with very little scent. Mango butter has a high content of stearic acid, which is similar to cocoa butter. It contributes to a conditioning bar of soap with a rich, creamy lather. It is typically used at 5% of the soap formula, or as a superfatting agent.

Mowrah Butter

INCI: *Bassia latifolia*

Label Name: Bassia latifolia (Mowrah) Seed Butter

SAP Value: .138

Melt Point: 97° F

Fatty Acids: 36% Oleic, 24% Palmitic, 22% Stearic, 15% Linoleic

Shelf Life: 1 year

Also called mahua butter, mowrah butter is derived from the kernels of the Mahua tree, which is native to India. It is a yellowish white butter with a mild scent, which is not noticeable in finished soap. It is used as a substitute for cocoa butter. In soap, it contributes to a hard, conditioning bar with creamy lather. Used as 3-6% of total fats and oils in a formula.

Murumuru Butter

INCI: *Astrocarya murumuru*

Label Name: Astrocaryum (Murumuru) Seed Butter

SAP Value: .196

Melt Point: 91° F

Fatty Acids: 47% Lauric, 26% Myristic, 15% Oleic, 6.% Palmitic, 3% Linoleic, 3% Stearic

Shelf Life: 1 year

Murumuru Butter is a yellowish white fat pressed from the fruit of the Murumuru tree, which is native to Brazil. Its fatty acid profile is similar to coconut oil. It is hard and has a waxy consistency. In soap, it contributes to a hard, cleansing bar with bubbly lather. Murumuru can be substituted for some of the coconut oil in your formula. Keep at below 30% of your total formula.

Palm Oil
INCI: Elaeis guineensis
Label Name: Elaeis guineensis (Palm) Oil
SAP Value: .139
Melt Point: 95° F
Fatty Acids: 44% Palmitic, 39% Oleic, 10% Linoleic, 5% Stearic, 1% Myristic
Shelf Life: 2 years
Palm oil comes from Palm trees, including the trunk and the leaves. Refined Palm oil is white and solid at room temperature. Palm oil is often substituted for tallow in all-vegetable formulas. Palm oil does not provide specific skin conditioning benefits; however, it is used in soaping due to its long shelf life and the fact that it contributes to a hard, white bar with stable lather. Palm oil can be drying, so use at no more than 30% of your formula.

There has been controversy surrounding the use of palm oil in soap due to the method in which the oil is harvested and the resulting effects on the environment and animals that depend upon the forests in which palm trees grow. In our Resource Directory, we list businesses that sell sustainable palm oil that does not contribute to deforestation.

Palm Kernel Oil
INCI: *Elaeis guineensis*
Label Name: Elaeis guineesis (Palm) Kernel Oil
SAP Value: .156
Melt Point: 75° F
Fatty Acids: 49% Lauric, 17% Myristic, 16% Stearic, 8% Palmitic, 4% Oleic
Shelf Life: 1 year
Palm Kernel oil comes from the same plant from which Palm oil is derived, but its composition and properties are different. It is obtained from the kernels of the fruit on the palm trees. Palm kernel oil can be used as a substitute for some of the coconut called for in your formula. In soap, palm kernel oil contributes to a hard, white bar with fluffy lather. Using too much palm kernel oil will make a drying bar, so keep this under 30% of your formula. Note that this oil can also speed up trace.

Sal Butter
INCI: *Shorea robusta*
Label Name: Shorea robusta (Sal) Butter
SAP Value: .132
Melt Point: 97° F
Fatty Acids: 44% Stearic, 40% Oleic, 6% Palmitic, 2% Linoleic
Shelf Life: 2 years
Sal butter comes from the fruit of the Sal tree in India. Sal butter has properties similar to mango butter. The butter is light colored and has a slight odor. It is solid at room temperature, but melts upon skin contact. Sal butter contributes to a hard, conditioning bar of soap with a stable lather. Use up to 5% of your formula or as a superfatting agent.

Shea Butter
INCI: *Butyrospermum parkii*
Label Name: Butyrospermum parkii (Shea) Fruit Butter
SAP Value: .126
Melt Point: 109° F
Fatty Acids: 48% Oleic, 40% Stearic, 6% Linolenic, 5% Palmitic
Shelf Life: 1 year
Shea butter, sometimes called shea nut butter, is derived from the fruit (nut) of the Shea tree. It is a solid butter that melts upon skin contact. In soap, shea contributes to a harder conditioning bar with a silky, stable lather. It contains a large percentage of ingredients that do not react with lye, and thus remain in the soap to nourish your skin. Use up to 25% of your formula, or as a superfatting agent.

Tallow
INCI: (Beef Tallow)
Label Name: Beef Tallow
SAP Value: .140
Melt Point: 98°
Fatty Acids: 36% Oleic, 28% Plamitic, 22% Stearic, 6% Myristic, 3% Linoleic, 2% Lauric, 1% Linolenic
Shelf Life: 2 years
Tallow is the fat rendered from suet-the hard, fatty tissue around the kidneys of cows, sheep, deer, etc. It is a hard oil with a long shelf life. It is considered an economical soaping oil that creates a hard, white, conditioning soap bar with a rich, stable lather. Tallow can increase trace. Tallow can make your soap bars brittle, so be sure to keep this at 40% or less of your formula.

Tucuma Butter
INCI: *Astrocaryum tucuma*
Label Name: Astrocaryum tucuma (Tucuma) Seed Butter
SAP Value: .170
Melt Point: 87° F
Fatty Acids: 48% Lauric, 23% Myristic, 13% Oleic, 6% Palmitic
Shelf Life: 2 years
Tucuma Butter is cold pressed from the seed of the Tucuma palm tree, which is native to Brazil. It is hard at room temperature, but it melts upon skin contact. Tucuma butter has a characteristic odor which some might find unpleasant, but is not noticeable in finished soap. Tucuma butter creates a hard, cleansing bar of soap with fluffy lather. Use up to 10% of your formula or as a superfatting agent.

Soft (Liquid) Oils/Butters:

Apricot Kernel Oil
INCI: *Prunus armeniaca*
Label Name: Prunus armeniaca (Apricot) Kernel Oil
SAP Value: .135
Fatty Acids: 66% Oleic, 27% Linoleic, 6% Palmitic
Shelf Life: 6 months - 1 year
Apricot kernel oil is cold pressed from the dried kernels of apricots. This pressing yields a light, silky oil that absorbs quickly into skin. Apricot kernel oil is good for all skin types, especially sensitive, dry and mature skin. In soap, it contributes to a conditioning bar, with a stable lather. It is often used as a superfatting oil. Note that apricot kernel oil has a short shelf life, and should be refrigerated after opening.

Argan Oil
INCI: *Argania spinosa*
Label Name: Argania spinosa (Argan) Nut Oil
SAP Value: .134
Fatty Acids: 46% Oleic, 34% Linoleic, 14% Palmitic, 1% Myristic, 1% Linolenic
Shelf Life: 2 years
Argan oil is a rare oil pressed from the fruits of the Argan tree, which is native to Morocco. It is called liquid gold for its deep golden color as well as its many nutritive, cosmetic and medicinal properties. Argan oil is high in antioxidants, and has a long shelf life. In soap, argan oil contributes to a conditioning bar of soap with a rich, stable lather. Use up to 10% of your formula or as a superfatting oil. DO NOT USE IF YOU HAVE NUT ALLERGIES.

Avocado Oil

INCI: *Persea gratissima*

Label Name: Persea gratissima (Avocado) Oil

SAP Value: .132

Fatty Acids: 58% Oleic, 20% Palmitic, 12% Linoleic, 2% Stearic

Shelf Life: 1 year

Avocado oil is pressed from the fleshy pulp that surrounds the avocado pit. It is a yellowish green oil, depending on the level of refining the oil has gone through. In soap, avocado oil creates a conditioning bar with mild cleansing properties that also has a stable, creamy lather. Avocado oil can be used up to 20% of your formula, and is especially good used as a superfatting oil.

Baobab Oil

INCI: *Adansonia digitata*

Label Name: Adansonia digitata (Baobab) Seed Oil

SAP Value: .143

Fatty Acids: 37% Oleic, 28% Linoleic, 24% Palmitic, 4% Stearic, 2% Linolenic, 1% Myristic

Shelf Life: 2 years

Baobab oil is cold pressed from the seeds of the Baobab tree, which is native to Eastern and Southern Africa. It is a thick, pale oil, with a faint sweet, nutty aroma that is not discernible in finished soap. Baobab contributes to a conditioning bar of soap. Use at 5% of your formula or as a superfatting oil.

Borage Oil

INCI: *Borago officinalis*

Label Name: Borago officinalis (Borage) Seed Oil

SAP Value: .130

Fatty Acids: 43% Linoleic, 20% Oleic, 10% Palmitic, 5% Linolenic, 4% Stearic

Shelf Life: 6 months

Borage Seed oil is an oil often used in anti-aging skin care formulations, but is not a popular soap making oil, due to its short shelf life. This oil must be stored in a cool, dark location, as light, heat and humidity all lead to the breakdown of the fragile oil. If used at all, we suggest incorporating borage seed oil as a superfatting agent, and be sure to incorporate antioxidants into your soap formula. It can contribute to a conditioning bar of soap with stable lather.

Brazil Nut Oil

INCI: *Bertholletia excelsa*

Label Name: Bertholletia excelsa (Brazil) Nut Oil

SAP Value: .138

Fatty Acids: 38% Linoleic, 38% Oleic, 15% Palmitic, 10% Stearic,

Shelf Life: 1 year

Brazil nut trees are native to the Amazon rainforest, and can live up to 700 years. Each mature tree produces up to 300 fruit pods per year, with each pod containing up to 25 nuts in individual shells. The clear, yellowish oil is extracted from the nuts and used in a variety of skin and hair care applications. Brazil nut oil contributes to a conditioning bar of soap. Use up to 5% of your formula or as a superfatting oil.

Canola Oil

INCI: *Brassica campestris*

Label Name: Brassica campestris (Canola) Oil

SAP Value: .123

Fatty Acids: 61% Oleic, 21% Linoleic, 9% Linoleic, 4% Palmitic, 2% Stearic

Shelf Life: 1 year

Canola oil is an economical oil often used as a substitute for olive oil in formulas. In soap, it creates a moisturizing bar with a stable creamy lather. It does make a very soft bar of soap, so be sure to use no more than 50% of your formula. Canola is slow to trace, so it is a good oil to use if you are coloring your soap and need a slow-moving formula to allow for time to swirl in colorants.

Castor Oil

INCI: *Ricinus communis*

Label Name: Ricinus communis (Castor) Seed Oil

SAP Value: .127

Fatty Acids: 90% Ricinoleic, 4% Linoleic, 4% Oleic

Shelf Life: 2 years

Castor Oil is pressed from the beans of the Castor plant. It is a thick, sticky oil containing a unique mixture of fatty acids. Castor oil is often used to make soap more emollient and moisturizing. It creates a soothing, protective layer on the skin. Castor oil creates a stable, bubbly lather with plentiful small bubbles. It creates a conditioning soap bar with mild cleansing properties. Using more than 5-10% in your formula will lead to a sticky, soft bar of soap and can lead to cracking while in the soap mold. If using castor oil as one of the primary oils in your formula (and not as a superfatting oil), note that it can speed up trace.

Corn Oil
INCI: *Zea mays*
Label Name: Zea Mays (Corn) Oil
SAP Value: .137
Fatty Acids: 51% Linoleic, 3% Oleic, 12% Palmitic, 2% Stearic, 1% Linolenic
Shelf Life: 6 months
Corn oil is sometimes used as an inexpensive substitute for olive oil in soap making. It can be used up to 15% of your formula, but note that it creates a soft bar of soap and due to its short shelf life can be prone to rancidity. Be sure to add antioxidants to your formula if using corn oil. Corn oil contributes to a moisturizing bar of soap with stable lather.

Cottonseed Oil
INCI: *Gossypium herbaceum*
Label Name: Gossypium herbaceum (Cottonseed) Oil
SAP Value: .138
Fatty Acids: 52% Linoleic, 18% Oleic, 13% Palmitic, 13% Stearic, 1% Linolenic
Shelf Life: 6 months - 1 year
Cottonseed oil is extracted from cotton plants after the cotton lint (fluff) has been removed. Cottonseed oil is often recognized as one of the primary ingredients (in hydrogenated form) of Crisco® shortening. The hydrogenated version of cottonseed oil can be used as a substitute for lard. Liquid cottonseed oil contributes to a conditioning bar of soap with stable lather. Use up to 10% of your formula, or as a superfatting agent. Cottonseed oil is prone to rancidity, so refrigerate after opening.

Flax Seed Oil
INCI: *Linum usitatissimum*
Label Name: Linum usitatissimum (Linseed) Seed Oil
SAP Value: .135
Fatty Acids: 50% Linolenic, 27% Oleic, 13% Linoleic, 6% Palmitic, 3% Stearic
Shelf Life: 6 months
Flax seed oil (also known as Linseed oil) is rich in Omega-3 essential fatty acids and is often used in skin care formulations. Flax seed oil is not commonly used in soap, due to its short shelf life. If you opt to use flax seed oil, add rosemary oleoresin extract to the oil, refrigerate the oil after opening, and use as a superfatting agent in a formula that contains other high antioxidant oils. Flax seed oil contributes to a softer bar of soap.

Grape Seed Oil
INCI: *Vitis vinifera*
Label Name: Vitis vinifera (Grape) Seed Oil
SAP Value: .134
Fatty Acids: 68% Linoleic, 20% Oleic, 8% Palmitic, 4% Stearic
Shelf Life: 3-6 months
Grape seed oil is a lightweight oil often used in anti-acne soap formulas due to its astringent properties. In soap, some say that it creates a unique creaminess to the lather. Grape seed oil is often used as a superfatting oil. It has a short shelf life, so treat with rosemary oleoresin extract and refrigerate the oil after opening. It can be used up to 5% in your formula, but be aware that the soap may go rancid quickly.

Hazelnut Oil
INCI: *Corylus avellana*
Label Name: Corylus avellana (Hazel) Seed Oil
SAP Value: .135
Fatty Acids: 75% Oleic, 10% Linoleic, 5% Palmitic, 3% Stearic
Shelf Life: 3-6 months
Hazelnut oil is a lightweight, strong smelling oil. It has a very short shelf life, and therefore is often only used in small amounts, if at all in soap formulas and usually as a superfatting ingredient. Hazelnut oil helps to create a conditioning bar with stable lather. If too much is used, the soap may be soft and prone to rancidity. Hazelnut oil is slow to trace. Due to its short shelf life, it is recommended that you keep Hazelnut oil stored in the refrigerator. DO NOT USE IF YOU HAVE NUT ALLERGIES.

Hemp Seed Oil
INCI: *Cannabis sativa*
Label Name: Cannabis sativa (Hemp) Seed Oil
SAP Value: .135
Fatty Acids: 57% Linoleic, 21% Linolenic, 12% Oleic, 6% Palmitic, 2 % Stearic
Shelf Life: 6 months
Hemp seed oil is a dark green oil with a distinct scent, though the scent is not noticeable in cured soap. It is a delicate oil with a short shelf life so we recommend keeping it refrigerated. Hemp seed oil can be used up to 15% in your soap formula, or as a superfatting agent. It contributes to a conditioning bar of soap with stable lather. It can also create a softer soap, with a slower trace. Because of its tendency to spoil, we suggest adding rosemary oleoresin extract to hemp seed oil and using it in small amounts to superfat your soap.

Jojoba Oil

INCI: *Simmondsia chinesis*

Label Name: Simmondsia chinesis (Jojoba) Seed Oil

SAP Value: .065

Fatty Acids: 12% Oleic

Shelf Life: 1+ years

Jojoba oil is not actually oil, but a liquid wax derived from the jojoba plant, which is native to the desert regions of the western United States. Jojoba is very similar to the oil secreted by our skin glands called sebum. Jojoba is excellent for oily or acne prone skin, as sebum dissolves in jojoba. Rich in Vitamin E, jojoba absorbs quickly and helps skin retain moisture. In soap, jojoba creates a stable lather. Jojoba also creates a conditioning bar of soap with mild cleansing properties. Use jojoba up to 10% of your base oils, or as a superfatting oil. Using more than 10% can decrease the lather in your finished bar of soap.

Kukui Nut Oil

INCI: *Aleurites moluccana*

Label Name: Aleurites moluccana (Kukui) Nut Oil

SAP Value: .135

Fatty Acids: 42% Linoleic, 29% Linolenic, 20% Oleic, 6% Palmitic, 2% Stearic

Shelf Life: 1 year

Kukui nut oil comes from the Kukui nut, which is native to Hawaii. Hawaiians have used it for centuries to protect and soothe their skin from the sun and salt water. In soap, kukui oil contributes to a moisturizing, conditioning bar of soap with stable lather. Use up to 10% in your formula, or as a superfatting agent. DO NOT USE IF YOU HAVE NUT ALLERGIES.

Macadamia Nut Oil

INCI: *Macadamia ternifolia*

Label Name: Macadamia ternifolia (Macadamia) Seed Oil

SAP Value: .137

Fatty Acids: 59% Oleic, 9% Palmitic, 5% Stearic, 2% Linoleic

Shelf Life: 1 year

Macadamia nut oil is a stable oil with high antioxidant properties that is most often used in skin-penetrating products such as lotions or creams. It has a light, nutty scent that is not noticeable in cured soap. In soap, it contributes to a conditioning, moisturizing bar with stable lather. Use as a superfatting agent. DO NOT USE IF YOU HAVE NUT ALLERGIES.

Meadowfoam Seed Oil

INCI: *Limnanthes alba*

Label Name: Limnanthes alba (Meadowfoam) Seed Oil

SAP Value: .119

Fatty Acids: 63% Eicosamic, 17% Erucic, 17% Docosadienoic, 1% Arachidic

Shelf Life: 2 years

Meadowfoam oil is a unique oil in that it contains over 98% fatty acids that have over 20 carbon atoms. It is a very stable oil, and is often used to help extend the shelf life of other, more fragile oils. Meadowfoam oil is most often used as a superfatting agent and contributes to a creamy lather in soap. If used as a primary oil in your soap formula, use at 20% or less.

Neem Oil

INCI: *Azadirachtin indica*

Label Name: Azadirachtin indica (Neem) Oil

SAP Value: .134

Fatty Acids: 50% Oleic, 18% Palmitic, 15% Stearic, 13% Linoleic

Shelf Life: 2 years

Neem oil has a potent, bitter aroma, which often discourages people from using it in their soap formulas. However, neem oil has a variety of uses from personal care to repelling insects, so it may be worth incorporating into your specialty soaps. Note that the scent is much less potent in finished soap, though depending upon the amount used may still be noticeable. We recommend starting with 5% of your formula and then increasing up to 10% if you do not find the scent in the cured soap unpleasant. Oftentimes, using a blend of earthy or woodsy essential oils or fragrance oils helps to cover/meld the neem scent into a pleasant blend. Neem contributes to a conditioning bar of soap with stable lather.

Olive Oil

INCI: *Olea europaea*

Label Name: Olea europaea (Olive) Fruit Oil

SAP Value: .133

Fatty Acids: 69% Oleic, 14% Palmitic, 12% Linoleic, 3% Stearic, 1% Linolenic

Shelf Life: 2 years

Olive oil is one of the most well-known soaping oils, renowned for its moisturizing and humectant properties. It is a mild oil that attracts moisture and helps the moisture penetrate deep into the skin. Olive oil comes from the pressing of olives. Pomace olive oil is the oil extracted from the very last pressing of the olives. It is the least expensive oil to use and produces a very mild, non-drying soap with a creamy lather. Though soaps made exclusively with olive oil are initially very soft, after an extra long (12 weeks) cure time, the soap is hard and long-lasting. Use up to 100% in your formula.

Peach Kernel Oil
INCI: *Prunus persica*
Label Name: Prunus persica (Peach) Kernel Oil
SAP Value: .136
Fatty Acids: 65% Oleic, 25% Linoleic, 6% Palmitic, 2% Stearic, 1% Linolenic
Shelf Life: 1 year
Peach kernel oil is a light oil, often used in cosmetics for mature or sensitive skin. In soap, it can be substituted for apricot kernel, sweet almond or grape seed oils. Use no more than 25% of your formula for a moisturizing, conditioning bar of soap with stable lather.

Peanut Oil
INCI: *Arachis hypogaea*
Label Name: Arachis hypogaea (Peanut) Oil
SAP Value: .137
Fatty Acids: 56% Oleic, 26% Linoleic, 8% Palmitic, 3% Stearic
Shelf Life: 6 months – 1 year
Peanut oil is not a popular oil in soap making due to its relatively short shelf life. It is typically used as a less expensive substitute for olive or canola oil. Peanut oil contributes to a conditioning, soft bar of soap with stable lather. Use no more than 25% of your formula. DO NOT USE IF YOU HAVE PEANUT ALLERGIES.

Rice Bran Oil
INCI: *Oryza sativa*
Label Name: Oryza sativa (Rice) Bran Oil
SAP Value: .129
Fatty Acids: 43% Oleic, 26% Linoleic, 22% Palmitic, 3% Stearic, 1% Myristic
Shelf Life: 1+ years
Rice bran oil comes from the bran and germ of brown rice. It is a mild oil high in fatty acids; perfect for dry/flaky skin. In soap, it results in a stable, creamy, conditioning lather with mild cleansing. In some formulas, the inclusion of rice bran oil can lead to an attractive sheen on the soap surface. Rice bran oil is often used as a less expensive substitute for olive oil in a soap recipe, and can be used up to 25% of the formula.

Safflower Oil
INCI: *Carthamus tinctorius*
Label Name: Carthamus tinctorius (Safflower) Seed Oil
SAP Value: .135
Fatty Acids: 75% Linoleic, 15% Oleic, 7% Palmitic
Shelf Life: 1 year
Safflower oil is very similar to soybean, canola and sunflower oils. Safflower oil is cold pressed from the seeds of the Safflower plant. It helps create a conditioning, moisturizing bar of soap with a stable lather. Use up to 20% of your soap formula. More than 20% will lead to a very soft bar of soap.

Sesame Oil
INCI: *Sesamum indicum*
Label Name: Sesamum indicum (Sesame) Seed Oil
SAP Value: .135
Fatty Acids: 43% Linoleic, 40% Oleic, 10% Palmitic, 5% Stearic
Shelf Life: 6 months - 1 year
Sesame oil is cold pressed from sesame seeds. It is a heavy oil with a strong nutty scent that is traditionally used in Ayurvedic medicine. In soap, it contributes to a moisturizing, conditioning bar of soap with stable lather. Using more than 10% in your formula can lead to a softer soap.

Soybean Oil
INCI: *Glycine soja*
Label Name: Glycine soja (Soybean) Oil
SAP Value: .134
Fatty Acids: 50% Linoleic, 24% Oleic, 11% Palmitic, 8% Linolenic, 5% Stearic
Shelf Life: 1 year
Soybean oil is an inexpensive, light oil that easily absorbs into the skin. In soap, it contributes to a hard slightly conditioning bar with a stable lather. Soybean oil is normally used as an inexpensive "filler oil" in conjunction with oils and butters that provide additional moisturizing and skin conditioning. It also helps to slow down trace. Use up to 50% of your formula. The use of hydrogenated soybean oil provides a harder bar, whereas non-hydrogenated soybean oil provides better conditioning but with slightly less lather. DO NOT USE IF YOU HAVE SOY ALLERGIES.

Sunflower Oil

INCI: *Helianthus annuus*

Label Name: Helianthus annuus (Sunflower) Seed Oil

SAP Value: .134

Fatty Acids: 83% Oleic, 4% Stearic, 4% Linoleic, 3% Palmitic, 1% Linolenic

Shelf Life: 6 months – 1 year depending on if you're using high oleic oil

Sunflower oil is an inexpensive, emollient-rich oil extracted from sunflower seeds. It is high in essential fatty acids and it is recommended for all skin types. Sunflower oil helps the skin to retain moisture and regenerate new cells. In soap, sunflower oil contributes to a conditioning bar with a silky feel and stable lather. Using more than 25% in your formula will create a soft bar of soap. Sunflower oil will slow trace down, so this is a good oil to include if you want to create swirls or other details in your soap that take time to create. Be sure to use high oleic sunflower oil, as it is naturally more stable and resistant to rancidity.

Sweet Almond Oil

INCI: *Prunus amygdalus dulcis*

Label Name: Prunus amygdalus dulcis (Sweet Almond) Oil

SAP Value: .137

Fatty Acids: 71% Oleic, 18% Linoleic, 7% Palmitic

Shelf Life: 1 year

This nutrient-rich oil is pressed from the dried kernels of the sweet almond. It is renowned for its ability to soften and condition the skin. In soap, sweet almond oil contributes to a conditioning, mildly cleansing, moisturizing bar with stable lather. Use sweet almond oil for up to 15% of your formula, or as a superfatting agent. DO NOT USE IF YOU HAVE NUT ALLERGIES.

Tamanu Oil

INCI: *Calophyllum inophyllum*

Label Name: Calophyllum inophyllum (Tamanu) Oil

SAP Value: .148

Fatty Acids: 38% Linoleic, 34% Oleic, 13% Stearic, 12% Palmitic, 1% Linolenic

Shelf Life: 2 years

Tamanu oil is made by crushing the dried nuts of the Tamanu tree, and has a very earthy, nutty scent. Tamanu has been used for centuries for a variety of skin ailments. It can be used as up to 5% of your soap formula, or as a superfatting oil. Tamanu contributes to a conditioning bar of soap. DO NOT USE IF YOU HAVE NUT ALLERGIES.

Walnut Oil
INCI: *Juglans regia*
Label Name: Juglans regia (Walnut) Seed Oil
SAP Value: .136
Fatty Acids: 60% Linoleic, 18% Oleic, 12% Linolenic, 7% Palmitic, 2% Stearic
Shelf Life: 3-6 months
Walnut oil is cold pressed directly from walnuts, and the oil is a pale yellow with a light, nutty scent that is not noticeable in soap. Due to its short shelf life, walnut oil is not often used in soap making. You can use it up to 15% in your soap formula, though we recommend using other oils high in antioxidants and perhaps adding some rosemary oleoresin extract to stave off oxidation a bit longer. In soap, it contributes to a conditioning bar. Refrigerate after opening. DO NOT USE IF YOU HAVE NUT ALLERGIES.

Watermelon Oil
INCI: *Citrullus vulgaris*
Label Name: Citrullus vulgaris (Watermelon) Seed Oil
SAP Value: .135
Fatty Acids: 60% Linoleic, 18% Oleic, 11% Palmitic, 10% Stearic
Shelf Life: 1+ years
Watermelon seed oil is also known as Ootanga oil or Kalahari oil. In Africa, watermelon seeds are removed from the rind and then allowed to dry outside in the sun. Once dried, the seeds are then pressed to extract the oil. As it is a mild oil, it is quite popular in baby products. Because it is a more exotic and expensive oil, it is often used just in small amounts in soap as a superfatting oil. In soap, watermelon oil contributes to a conditioning bar with stable lather.

Wheat Germ Oil
INCI: *Triticum vulgare*
Label Name: Triticum vulgare (Wheat) Germ Oil
SAP Value: .135
Fatty Acids: 58% Linoleic, 17% Oleic, 17% Palmitic, 2% Stearic
Shelf Life: 1 year
Wheat germ oil is a thick, slightly sticky oil with a distinct smell. It is nature's richest source of Vitamin E, and as a result, has very high antioxidant properties. Wheat germ oil is often added to other oils to extend their shelf life. In soap, Wheat germ oil creates a stable lather and conditioning soap bar. Use up to 15% in your formula. Refrigerate after opening. DO NOT USE IF YOU HAVE WHEAT OR GLUTEN ALLERGIES.

Superfatting

Superfatting is an additional amount of oil in a formula that is calculated to <u>not</u> saponify. The excess molecules of oil do not have lye with which to bond, which contributes to a more gentle and less drying bar of soap.

You can use a lye calculator (discussed in Chapter 14) to calculate a superfat, which is also called a lye discount because you're discounting or reducing the amount of lye needed to bond with every oil molecule. Most soap makers will use between a 3 and 8 percent superfat, with the average being 5%. If you have more than a 10 percent superfat, your soap may be soft and prone to going rancid.

Superfatting can be obtained by:

1. Reducing the amount of lye in the formula so only a portion of the oils in the formula are saponified OR
2. Adding additional oils to the formula after trace. Since there are no extra sodium hydroxide molecules left, the additional oils that are added do not saponify, providing superfat to the soap.

"It is personal preference on whichever method you choose to follow. Some prefer to follow the pre-trace (option #1) above so they don't accidentally forget to add the superfatting oil. Others save their exotic or more expensive oils for the post-trace (option #2). I have used both approaches, with no differences noted in the final soap. I personally like a 5 to 7 percent superfat in my formulas." - Alyssa

CHAPTER 4
USING ALTERNATIVE LIQUIDS IN SOAP

There are a variety of alternative liquids that can be used in making soap. There are also particular benefits and special considerations or steps needed when using certain liquids. We dedicate the entire next chapter to making goat milk soap, and in this chapter we'll discuss liquids including coffee, tea, wine, beer and other liquors.

Coffee

Coffee is often used in soap to add color and scent. It is most often used full strength or double or triple strength.

Additional Equipment Needed

To use coffee as your liquid, you need a coffee maker in which water passes through the ground coffee in a filter and drips into a pot.

Steps

Oftentimes, a single brew is not strong enough in color to survive the saponification process, so we recommend using a double or even triple brew. To create 3 cups (24 ounces) of a triple strength coffee, follow these steps:

1. Place enough distilled water and coffee grounds in the coffee maker to make 3 cups of coffee. Run the coffee cycle as usual.

2. When the coffee is finished brewing, discard the used coffee grounds and add to a new filter a second quantity of coffee sufficient to make 3 cups of coffee.

3. Instead of adding fresh water to the coffee maker, pour the already brewed coffee into the coffee maker. Run the coffee cycle again.

4. When the coffee is finished brewing, you now have double strength coffee. Repeat steps 2 and 3, and you'll have triple strength coffee.

5. Use the desired amount of triple strength coffee in the liquid portion of your soap formula once the coffee has cooled to room temperature.

Mocha Coffee Soap Formula

Pomace olive oil	8.00 ounces
Coconut oil	4.00 ounces
Shea butter	3.20 ounces
Castor oil	0.80 ounces
Coffee (double strength brew)	5.60 ounces
Sodium hydroxide	2.20 ounces
Used coffee grounds	½ Tablespoon
Cocoa powder	½ Tablespoon

There are a number of wonderful coffee or mocha coffee fragrance oils that can be added to this soap to bump up the scent. Alternatively, you can omit the coffee grounds if you don't want an exfoliating bar of soap.

Tea

Tea is also used in soap as an alternative liquid to add color and scent.

Additional Equipment Needed

Tea pot
Heat-resistant container in which to steep the tea
Tea in a tea bag or loose tea in a tea ball

Steps

Tea also often requires a long and/or a double strength steep. There are a few ways in which you can do this. To create 3 cups (24 ounces) of a double strength tea, follow these steps:

1. Boil 3 cups of distilled water.

2. When the water is boiling, pour it into the heat-resistant container. Add 6 tea bags (twice as many bags as needed for 3 cups) and let steep for 20 minutes.

3. Strain the tea bags and use the tea in the liquid portion of your soap formula.

You can also use the double brew coffee method:
1. Boil 3 cups of distilled water.

2. When the water is boiling, pour it into the heat-resistant container. Add 3 tea bags and let steep for 20 minutes.

3. Strain the tea bags and discard them.

4. Pour the tea back into the teapot and bring to a boil again.

5. Pour the boiling tea back into the heat-resistant container. Add 3 new tea bags and let steep for 20 minutes.

6. Strain the tea bags and use the tea as the liquid portion of your soap formula once it has cooled to room temperature.

Triple Peppermint Soap Formula

Pomace olive oil	8.00 ounces
Coconut oil	4.00 ounces
Shea butter	3.20 ounces
Castor oil	0.80 ounces
Peppermint tea (double strength brew)	5.60 ounces
Sodium hydroxide	2.20 ounces
Peppermint essential oil	0.50 ounces
Finely crushed peppermint leaves	1 Teaspoon

Wine

Wine is used to impart color and boost lather in soap. Some things to remember when soaping with wine:

To avoid overheating of the formula, do not use wine as your only liquid. Instead, mix it with distilled water in your formula.

You must soap 'cold', meaning that the liquids must be kept as cool as possible to avoid the volcano effect when mixing the lye with the wine.

The scent of the wine will not be noticeable in the final soap.

Wine may color the soap slightly, and may result in an off-color such as tan. You may want to use an oil infused with a natural colorant like madder root or alkanet powder to create a light pink to burgundy color, or include a rose colored clay. We discuss natural colorants and clay in Chapters 7 and 9, respectively.

Additional Equipment Needed
Heat-resistant container in which to simmer the wine
Pot to create a double boiler system with the heat-resistant container

Steps

Wine must have the majority of the alcohol removed from it before being used in soap. If this is not done you may experience a dangerous volcano effect when mixing and pouring the soap.

1. Pour wine into the heat-resistant container. Pour in about two times as much as you'd like to use in your formula. For instance, if you want to use 6 ounces of wine in your formula, then pour 12 ounces into the container.

2. Add water to the pot and turn heat on medium to medium high. Put the heat-resistant container into the pot to create a double boiler system.

3. Let the wine simmer for approximately 30 minutes. Quite a bit of the wine will evaporate as it reduces, which is why you've poured in twice as much as your formula calls for. Never leave wine unattended while simmering. Due to the alcohol content it is very prone to boiling dry, scorching, and to catching fire.

4. At the end of the simmer, set wine aside to cool. If possible, let it sit overnight, keep it in the refrigerator, or freeze it and break it into slushy chunks prior to mixing it with distilled water (when used as part of the lye solution).

When it is time to soap, you can go one of two routes: include the wine as part of the lye solution or add the wine at trace. Adding it at trace will reduce the likelihood of a volcano effect occurring. The instructions for each method are listed below.

As part of the lye solution

1. Measure out your desired amount of wine. Add it to the amount of distilled water to create the required amount of liquid for your formula. Place this container into an ice bath to keep it chilled.

2. **Slowly** add lye and stir, making sure the solution does not overheat. Add a very small amount of lye, stir, let it rest, and then repeat. This is a slow process to ensure the mixture does not overheat.

3. When the lye solution has been mixed, continue with standard soap making procedures.

At trace

1. The water used to make the lye solution will be discounted by the amount of wine you'll be using. For instance, if your formula calls for 20 ounces of water and you want to use 6 ounces of reduced wine, then measure 14 ounces of distilled water to create the lye solution.

2. Follow standard soap making procedures, using extreme caution because the lye solution is concentrated and even more caustic.

3. At light trace, pour in the reduced wine along with any exfoliants, scents, etc.

4. Continue with standard soap making procedures.

Wine Soap Formula

This formula is especially nice if you use some alkanet-infused olive oil (see pages 68-71) to naturally color the soap and scent with a wine scented fragrance oil.

Palm oil	5.52 ounces
Coconut oil	4.43 ounces
Pomace olive oil	4.43 ounces
Shea butter	2.23 ounces
Sodium hydroxide	2.18 ounces
Distilled water	2.61 ounces
Wine	2.60 ounces

Beer

Beer is used in soap to add color, scent, and to boost lather. Some notes to remember when soaping with beer:

You must soap 'cold', meaning that the beer must be kept as cool as possible to avoid the volcano effect when mixing with lye.

The scent of the beer may not be noticeable in the final soap.

Beer may color the soap slightly depending upon the hops and other ingredients in the beer.

Additional Equipment Needed

Heat-resistant container in which to simmer the beer
Pot to create a double boiler system with the heat-resistant container

Steps

Beer contains carbonation, which can be dangerous when mixed with lye, so it must always be flat before being used in a soap formula. If flat beer is not used you may experience a dangerous volcano effect when mixing the lye solution or pouring the soap into the mold.

There are two ways to flatten beer. Use whichever method is easiest for you and fits into your schedule.

To flatten beer

1. Measure and pour the beer into a container with a wide opening to enable air and bubbles to escape.

2. Allow the beer to sit for at least 24 hours, which allows it to go flat. Store the container of beer in a refrigerator if you leave it open for several days to prevent mold. Once the beer is flat, you may also freeze it to prevent it from overheating when the lye is added.

Note: You may also follow the steps recommended for boiling wine on page 52 if you do not want to wait for the beer to naturally go flat.

3. Slowly add lye to the room temperature, cold, or frozen beer and stir, making sure the solution does not overheat. Add a very small amount of lye, stir, let it rest, and repeat. This is a slow process to ensure the mixture does not overheat.

4. When the lye solution has been mixed, continue with standard soap making procedures.

<u>Beer Soap Formula</u>

Citrus Beer Soap   Note: a light beer works best in this formula.

Pomace olive oil	5.60 ounces
Coconut oil	4.80 ounces
Palm oil	4.80 ounces
Castor oil	0.80 ounces
Flat beer	5.12 ounces
Sodium hydroxide	2.29 ounces
Orange peel powder	½ teaspoon
Listea cubeba essential oil	0.20 ounces
Sweet orange essential oil	0.40 ounces
Grapefruit essential oil	0.40 ounces

Other Liquors

Soap makers are by nature curious and experimental, and want to try and incorporate just about anything they can into a soap formula. Our research uncovered soap makers who have tried to use other liquors such as vodka, gin, whiskey, etc. into soap, but we were unable to find any evidence of successful batches. We suspect this is due to the high sugar and alcohol content in liquor, which leads to either a volcano effect or seizing of the mixture.

Tips

Most wine, and some types of beer, do not scent the soap. There are excellent wine fragrances on the market that will enhance wine soap. Many soap makers include beer in their shaving and shampoo soaps. You may consider essential oils that further enhance the properties of the beer-based soap.

"I often receive the question: Do you create a new formula for each type of soap that you sell? My answer is no. Once I develop a formula that my customers love I use it for most of the soaps that I sell. For example, when I make wine soap I substitute wine for the goat milk in the formula. When other ingredients are added, such as clay, I simply add the clay to my existing formula. Experimentation is fun, but it can be expensive when operating a business. A tried and true formula, one that you use over and over again, saves both time and money." - Mary

CHAPTER 5
GOAT MILK SOAP

In this chapter we guide you through our method of making luxurious and creamy goat milk soap. The key element to a successful batch of goat milk soap is to keep the ingredients from overheating, which requires a lengthier production time.

Introduction to Goat Milk

Goat milk has a unique molecular structure, making it well-suited for people with allergic reactions to other types of milk. Goat milk is high in proteins, vitamins, and minerals. The silky lather of goat milk soap tends to be much less drying than other types of soap formulas.

Excerpt from AnniesGoatHill.com:

Breaking Down Goat Milk - Caprylic Acid

In personal care products and soaps there are many different types of "acids" that are beneficial for the health of a person's skin, one of which is caprylic acid.

What is caprylic acid?

Caprylic acid is a fatty acid found in the milk of many mammals, with goat milk containing one of the highest percentages. It can also be found in coconut and palm kernel oil. Caprylic acid is very easily digested and absorbed.

What is a fatty acid?

In non-chemistry terms, a fatty acid is a major component of fats that is used by the body for energy and tissue development (skin being of great importance), a major component of cellular lipids (lipids are fats that are very important to our bodies - they can help lubricate the joints, boost brain function, assist with fighting off fungal infections, and promote vitamin absorption). A body cannot generate its own fatty acids, they must be ingested via nutrition or a supplement.

Ways You Can Find Goat Milk

Raw goat milk can be purchased directly from farmers. Goat milk can also be purchased in many grocery stores, usually found in the organic and specialty dairy sections of the store. Goat milk can also be purchased canned and in dehydrated (powdered) form as well. Both can be found at the grocery store or through soap and cosmetic supply distributors which are listed in our Resource Directory at the end of this book.

To find farms that supply goat milk, contact your local agriculture extension office, a local goat club, your state dairy goat association, or the American Dairy Goat Association (www.adga.org).

Types of Goat Milk and How To Use Them in Soap

Raw Goat Milk in Soap
To make soap using raw goat milk you'll simply freeze the milk (or water and milk if desired), then add it to your formula as instructed below.

Canned Goat Milk in Soap
Canned goat milk is fairly easy to find on the grocery store shelf, often near other milk products used in baking, such as evaporated milk or condensed milk. To use canned goat milk, first shake the can well before opening. Then open the can and pour the milk into an ice cube tray. Freeze until slushy or solid, then add to your formula as instructed in the steps below.

Note: Condensed milk has been reduced, therefore, you may want to thin the milk down by adding 25 to 50% liquids (distilled water). E.g.: 4 ounce condensed milk, add 1 to 2 ounces of water.

Powdered Goat Milk in Soap
Powdered goat milk is not as easy to find in the grocery store, but some markets will carry powdered goat milk right next to the canned version. There are also a number of online suppliers where powdered goat milk can be purchased. See our Resource Directory for a listing of recommended ingredient suppliers.

To use powdered goat milk, follow the dilution instructions on the package. On average, the ratio is 1 tablespoon of powdered goat milk to 2 ounces of water. Mix the powder and water together until fully reconstituted. You can then pour the milk into ice cube trays and place in the freezer. Freeze until slushy or solid, then add to your formula as instructed in the steps below.

In this book we're focusing on using a mixture of goat milk and water. We recommend starting your goat milk soaping by using a formula that uses 50% water and 50% goat milk. As a reminder, we recommend distilled water, which is inexpensive and is easily found at the grocery store. Distilled water is better to use than regular tap water, since distilled water does not contain any impurities.

The most important step that you will learn in making goat milk soap is to keep the liquids (milk and water) at the coolest possible temperature while mixing in the lye. For this reason, we recommend freezing the milk and water in preparation for soap making. Freeze the liquids in pans, leak proof bags, or ice cube trays to enable the liquids to be easily broken into chunks for soap making.

Steps to Making Goat Milk Soap

Making cold process soap with goat milk is a more complicated and lengthier process compared to making soap with just distilled water due to the necessity of keeping the ingredients at a low temperature. Keeping the liquids at a low temperature ensures the milk does not scorch. The making of cold process soap, in general, is a precise process, since a chemical reaction takes place. Inaccurate measurements of the ingredients could easily cause the batch to fail.

We'll go through the steps to make soap with a formula that includes both goat milk and water. Gradually build up the amount of goat milk that you include in your recipes, and decrease the amount of water, as you become accustomed to making soap that contains goat milk.

Additional Equipment Needed
Stainless steel strainer
Distilled Water

Steps
1. Prepare your molds.

2. Put on all of your safety gear.

3. Set out all of the utensils and equipment needed for making soap.

4. Weigh your lye into a glass or heavy plastic container. Set the container aside.

5. Measure out all of the ingredients, except for the frozen milk and water.

6. Slowly begin heating the oils. Heat the solid oils and butters first, removing the pan from the heat while the solid oils are partially melted. Add liquid oils to the partially melted solid oils. This will ensure the temperature of your oils remain at a low temperature.

7. Break the frozen milk (or milk and distilled water) into large chunks and weigh the correct amount into a glass or heavy plastic pitcher or other container with a pouring spout.

8. **Slowly** pour a dusting of the measured lye onto the frozen milk and water chunks. The lye will cause a chemical reaction which begins to melt the frozen liquids. Hand stir the mixture.

9. Carefully sprinkle a little more lye onto the frozen liquid and lye mixture and slowly hand stir. Allow the mixture to rest until the chunks stop melting. If you notice a small amount of yellow liquid forming (indicating a warm pocket in the lye and milk), gently hand stir to distribute the overheated portion of your mixture.

Note: this is a **slow** process, with the goal of not overheating the lye and milk mixture. There are three steps involved in step 9: **gradually** add the lye to the milk and water chunks, hand stir gently, and allow the mixture to rest. Once the chunks stop melting, repeat the three steps. You may also set the mixing container into a bowl of ice to prevent the mixture from overheating.

Each time you repeat the three steps you will notice the chunks melting, eventually they will melt into a liquid that resembles watered down milk.

10. The chunks are now melted into a creamy white liquid.

11. Check the temperature of the oils and milk. Both should be at 90°F or lower. If the temperature of the lye solution is above 90°F, place the mixing container into an ice bath to reduce the temperature.

12. Using a stainless steel strainer as a filter, pour the milk and lye mixture into the oils. The strainer will catch any solids that have formed during the mixing process. The fats and cream in the milk may react to lye by forming solids that resemble a finely textured creamy white cottage cheese. You may push the fats through the strainer, or you can discard them. Bright yellow or orange spots are un-dissolved lye particles; do not push them through the strainer. Discard them with caution.

13. Begin mixing the lye solution and oils with your stick blender. Slowly move the stick blender through the mixture to thoroughly combine all of the ingredients.

14. As you feel and see the mixture getting thicker, test the mixture for 'trace'. This is when you turn off the stick blender, lift it out of the mixture and let the soap on the blender head dribble into the mixture below. If the drops sit on top of the mixture for a moment before sinking in, you have reached trace. This may be a very fast process or may take a while, depending on the oils used in your formula. Stop mixing at this point. You do not want to have thick trace (where the mixture looks like pudding), as this might make it difficult to add in fragrance and/or additives.

15. Add in any additives and superfatting oil(s). Stir slightly with the stick blender to disperse the additives throughout the mixture.

16. Add in the fragrance or essential oils, and any other additives and stir again with the stick blender until everything is mixed well.

17. Your soap will be thicker now, almost pudding consistency. It is now ready to be poured into your prepared mold.

18. When all the soap has been poured into the mold, place a layer of plastic wrap on top of the soap. Protecting the soap from exposure to air helps to prevent a white film from forming on the soap. The white film is often referred to as soda ash.

19. Insulating or wrapping the mold in towels or small blankets to keep the temperature of the soap from cooling too quickly, is <u>not</u> necessary with goat milk soap. The sugar and protein content in goat milk speeds up the saponification process, which in turn speeds up the heating of the soap mixture itself. If the room conditions are drafty or cool, below average room temperature, insulate the soap mold lightly.

20. After about 24 hours, your soap will be firm in the mold. Carefully remove the soap log from the mold. If you have difficulties in releasing your soap from the mold, it may need more time in the mold. Let it sit for another 12-24 hours. If after that time you still cannot get the soap out of the mold, then refer to the mold manufacturer's website to see what they recommend with their particular mold. Follow manufacturer's directions, so that you do not damage your mold.

21. Cut your soap into bars. Newly-made goat milk soap may emit an odor similar to ammonia. After a couple of days on the curing rack, the ammonia smell, if present at first, will dissipate.

22. Place your cut bars onto a rack to cure. Let the soap cure for at least 4-6 weeks. We also recommend locating the curing rack in a room with average to low humidity, and using a de-humidifier is very helpful when drying goat milk soaps, which may take longer to cure than water based soaps.

23. Voila! Your soaps are ready.

Sample Goat Milk Soap Formulas

Castile Goat Milk Soap, Single Oil Formula

Pomace olive oil	16.60 ounces
Sodium hydroxide	2.19 ounces
Distilled water	2.61 ounces
Goat milk	2.60 ounces

This Castile soap is gentle, easy to make, and because there are no additives such as fragrance or essential oil, the recipe normally produces a soap that hardens quickly. Castile soap is simple, making it a great formula for a person to use when learning how to make goat milk soap.

Annie's Luxurious Goat Milk Soap Formula

Palm oil	5.52 ounces
Coconut oil	4.43 ounces
Pomace olive oil	4.43 ounces
Shea butter	2.23 ounces
Sodium hydroxide	2.18 ounces
Distilled water	2.61 ounces
Goat milk	2.60 ounces

While you are learning how to make goat milk soap, we recommend using a formula that contains a balance of 50% distilled water and 50% goat milk. If you experience problems with your finished soap, refer to the troubleshooting section of this book where we recommend reducing the goat milk to 25% and increasing the distilled water to 75% of the formula. We do not recommend increasing the liquid to 100% goat milk until you have made several successful batches of goat milk soap.

"When making goat milk soap, the color of the milk as it melts should be creamy white. If the milk turns yellow or orange the mixture has overheated. This is caused by adding too much lye at once, and can also result from not hand mixing well enough. Until you have mastered the process of mixing lye with milk, have an ice bath on hand to set the mixing container in. You can use the yellow or orange milk mixture in your formula once it has cooled to the desired temperature, but it may result in tan, light brown, or yellow finished soap.

I prefer freezing my milk in shallow pans. I break the frozen liquids into large chunks before I weigh them for the formula. I have also used gallon sized freezer bags and ice cube trays." - Mary

CHAPTER 6
USING HERBS IN SOAP

Herbs can be wonderful additions to soap. Herbs can be used to provide additional scent, color or exfoliation properties. Herbs such as lavender, peppermint and chickweed have been used for centuries to soothe or treat various skin conditions.

Below are descriptions of commonly used herbs in soap. As we are not herbalists, we will not go into the properties, benefits or traditional medicinal uses of these herbs, but rather focus on *how the herbs look and act in soap*. Both of us regularly incorporate herbs into our soap formulas and recommend that you research each herb for your own personal usage.

The formulas in this book use dried herbs, not fresh. Water content in fresh herbs might foster the growth of mold and bacteria, so it is best to only use fully dried herbs in your soap formulas.

Herbs Commonly Used in Soap Making

Calendula
INCI: *Calendula officinalis*
Label: Calendula officinalis (Calendula) Flower Petals
Calendula is a perennial flower that is native to the Mediterranean region. The name refers to its tendency to bloom throughout the calendar - about once a month or with each new moon. Infused oils with calendula petals can help impart a soft golden yellow color to the finished soap. The petals add visual appeal to the finished soap and calendula petals are one of the few botanicals that retain its color through the saponification process.

Chamomile, German or Chamomile, Roman
INCI: *Chamomilla recutita, Anthemis nobilis*
Label: Chamomilla recutita (Chamomile) Flower or Anthemis nobilis (Chamomile) Flower
Chamomile is one of the most popular herbs used in soap and body care products due to its soothing, calming aroma. If used in powder form in soap, it creates a light beige speckled appearance. Note that chamomile is in the ragweed family, so if you are allergic to ragweed, then you should avoid using chamomile.

Chickweed
INCI: *Stellaria media*
Label: Stellaria media (Chickweed) Herb
Chickweed is a prolific herb that is reputed to be found in every region of the world. It even grows in the North Arctic Regions. Rich in minerals, this herb is often used in herbal medicine for poultices and skin irritations. Chickweed is most often used in an oil infusion in soap. It does not impart much, if any color to the finished soap.

Comfrey
INCI: *Symphytum officinale*
Label: Symphytum officinale (Comfrey) Leaf or Root Powder
Comfrey is known as one of the greatest medicinal herbs. It has been used in traditional Chinese medicine for over 2,000 years for inflamed and sensitive skin conditions. Besides infusing comfrey into oil, the leaf can also be ground and used to naturally produce a green bar of soap. Avoid using soap that contains comfrey on broken skin.

Lavender
INCI: *Lavandula angustifolia* or *Lavandula officinalis*
Label: Lavandula angustifolia (Lavender) Buds
One of the most recognized herbs, lavender is renowned to soothe nervous tension and promote restful sleep. Note that the color and fragrance of the herb will not survive the saponification process. Using lavender powder creates a bluish grey bar of soap. We do not recommend using lavender buds within the soap, as they discolor to an unsightly brown. Instead, press them into the top of the finished bar of soap to decorate.

Marshmallow Root
INCI: *Althaea officinalis*
Label: Althaea officinalis (Marshmallow Root) Powder
Marshmallow root has been used as a healing herb for thousands of years. In fact, Homer's *Iliad*, written over 2,800 years ago refers to its healing properties. It was widely used in traditional Greek medicine, and remains popular in Ayurvedic treatments. Marshmallow root is best extracted in water. Soak the root overnight, as this will create the best mucilaginous consistency (this is what provides the finished soap with a good 'slip' or 'glide') and use as part of the water called for in your formula. Marshmallow root is a common ingredient in shampoo soap bars. The slip it provides helps to detangle hair.

Plantain

INCI: *Plantago major*

Label: Plantago major (Plantain) Leaf Extract

Plantain is another well-known herb that has been used for centuries. The Saxons considered plantain as one of their nine sacred herbs. It is known in folklore as "Green Bandage," since it is one of the best poultice herbs available. Plaintain infused oil may help naturally color your soap green, depending upon how much of the infused oil is used.

Rooibos

INCI: *Aspalathus linearis*

Label: Aspalathus linearis (Rooibos) Leaf Extract

The rooibos plant is native to South Africa, and has been used in traditional African medicine for centuries. Rooibos contains strong antioxidant properties, which has led to its growing popularity in skin care products. Depending on the amount of infused oils used in your formula, rooibos infused oil may naturally color your soap a reddish brown color.

Rose

INCI: *Rose damascena* or *Rosa centifolia*

Label: Rose damascena (Rose) Petals

Roses are renowned worldwide for their beauty and exquisite fragrance. Rose petals are used to encourage relaxation and promote sweet dreams. Rose essential oil is rather pricey, since it takes about 60,000 roses to create just 1 ounce of essential oil. This is why many soap makers prefer to use the dried petals in their products – they are much less expensive and still provide beautiful decoration when pressed into the top of finished soap bars. We do not recommend using fresh rose petals in your soap formulas, as the petals do not retain their color through the saponification process and instead turn a rather unsightly brown.

Slippery Elm

INCI: *Ulmus fulva*

Label: Ulmus fulva (Slippery Elm) Bark Extract

Slippery Elm is a North American tree whose inner bark, when combined with water, creates a mucilaginous substance. Native Americans used to soak slippery elm bark in water and then place over wounds to dry as a natural bandage. For best results, soak the powder in water overnight to create the mucilaginous consistency and use as a portion of the water called for in your formula.

Yarrow
INCI: *Achillea millefolium*
Label: Achillea millefolium (Yarrow) Flowers
Yarrow is often referred to as the "Warrior Herb" due to its history of use in herbal medicine to clean and heal wounds and infections. Infused oil is a yellow color, although this color does not remain in the finished soap. Yarrow is not recommended while pregnant. Note that yarrow is in the ragweed family, so if you are allergic to ragweed, then you should avoid using yarrow as well.

Using Herbs in Soap
There are three ways in which you can use herbs in your soap formulas: using the powdered herb, infusing into water and infusing into oil.

Powder: Grind the herb into a fine powder. Add at light trace and mix well to add exfoliation properties to the soap bar. Just be sure to buy an inexpensive coffee bean grinder and use it only for grinding herbs. This way, your herbs won't smell like coffee and your coffee won't taste like herbs!

Water: Create a tea with the herb, and use it as the water amount of your soap formula. Refer to page 50 for instructions.

Oil: There are three methods in which you can create herb-infused oil, all of which are explained below. The method you use will depend on personal preference and/or how much time you have.

Making Infused Oils

Method #1 - Windowsill Method

You will need
1 cup dried herbs
2 cups olive oil
Glass Mason type jar
Cheesecloth, muslin or unbleached coffee filter
Sieve
Jar in which to store filtered oil

Steps
1. Place herbs into glass Mason type jar.

2. Pour oil over herbs. Oil should completely cover the herbs, and then some. If more oil is needed, add it to the jar and seal the lid.

3. Place the jar in a warm area (i.e., a windowsill in direct sunlight) for 48 hours to let the herbs steep in the oil.

4. At the end of the steep, place cheesecloth, muslin or an unbleached coffee filter into a sieve and filter the oil into a clean and dry jar.

5. Squeeze the cheesecloth/muslin/filter well to extract as much oil as possible.

6. Use the infused oil as a portion of or all of your oil in your soap formula.

Method #2 - Slow Cooker/Double Boiler

You will need
Slow cooker or double boiler
2 cup dried herbs
4 cups olive oil
Cheesecloth, muslin or unbleached coffee filter
Sieve
Jar in which to store filtered oil

Steps
1. Place herbs into slow cooker/double boiler.

2. Pour oil over herbs and stir mixture gently.

3. Slowly heat the herbs. Do not let the temperature of the mixture exceed 120°F (50°C). Any higher than 120°F and you will cook the herbs and oil.

4. Let the herbs steep for 2 hours, stirring every 30 minutes or so.

5. Turn off the slow cooker or remove the double boiler and let oil cool.

6. Place cheesecloth, muslin or an unbleached coffee filter into a sieve and filter the oil into a clean and dry jar.

7. Squeeze the cheesecloth/muslin/filter well to extract as much oil as possible.

8. Use the infused oil as a portion of or all of your oil in your soap formula.

Method #3-Tea Bag in Water Bath

This method places powdered herbs into sealed tea bags to eliminate the need for straining. The proportions are slightly different in this method to accommodate for available space in the canning jars.

You will need

2 Tablespoons powdered herbs
2/3 cup olive oil
Heat sealable tea bag
Iron
Canning jar and lid (½ pint or jam jar size)
Large cooking pot or slow cooker

Steps

1. Place herbs into heat sealable tea bag.

2. Seal the open edge with a hot iron. Be sure that the tea bag is fully sealed and set aside to cool (just takes a few moments).

3. Place the sealed tea bag into the canning jar.

4. Pour olive oil over tea bag to fully cover.

5. Attach the screw top lid to the canning jar, sealing it tightly.

6. If making multiple herbal infusions at the same time, use the permanent marker to write the name of the herb on the top of the sealed canning jar.

7. Place the jar into the large cooking pot or slow cooker. Fill the slow cooker with water until the water level is about ¾ as tall as the canning jars. You want to keep the water away from the lids of the jars so no water gets into the infusion.

8. If using a cooking pot, place on the stove top and turn the heat to low. If using a slow cooker, turn the setting to warm.

9. Let the herbs steep for 2 hours.

10. At the end of the steep, remove the jar from the pot or slow cooker and place on a towel on a counter top. Cover loosely with another towel for added protection while cooling. (Glass jars that are hot and then placed in a cool area can shatter due to the change in temperature.)

11. After the jar has cooled, remove the tea bag from the oil and squeeze gently to release as much infused oil as possible. Take care not to break the tea bag or you'll have to strain the oil to remove the powdered herbs.

12. Use the infused oil as either a portion of or all of your oil in your soap formula.

Using herb-infused oils does not change the information entered into a lye calculator. For instance, if you infuse calendula petals into olive oil, you simply select "olive oil" in the lye calculator.

Variations

- Use a combination of herbs in the infusion to incorporate different soothing properties from each herb.

- Make double-strength infusions by taking the infused oils and adding a new set of herbs and repeat the infusion process again. This will strengthen the amount of nutrients in the infused oil.

- Use oils with a stable shelf life such as jojoba, high oleic sunflower, coconut, etc.

CHAPTER 7
COLORING YOUR SOAP

There are a number of ways in which you can color your soap: herbs, micas, ultramarines, dioxides and FD&C colorants. In this chapter we'll discuss each and provide simple, step-by-step instructions for creating beautiful soaps with these coloring options.

Coloring Using Herbal Infusions

Herbs can impart a lovely color to your soap, but please note that the FDA has not approved herbs specifically as a coloring agent. You may color your soap with herbs, and list the herbs on the soap label, but do not list them specifically as a colorant. Coloring your soaps using herbs is a fairly straightforward process. Simply follow the instructions from pages 68-71 to make an herbal oil infusion. Start with a light colored oil, such as sunflower or olive oil and infuse the herb of choice into the oil. When the oil is strained, you'll see the oil has taken on the color of the herb or botanical. Use this infused, colored oil as part of your formula. For instance, if your formula calls for 10 ounces of olive oil, replace up to the total 10 ounces with the infused olive oil. You will need to experiment with this technique to find the exact amount to use to achieve the shade of color that you're looking for. Be sure to take detailed notes so that once you find the perfect shade of color, you'll know how to recreate it.

> "If you have never colored soap with herbs before, here's an example that you can use as reference: For a 2 pound batch of lavender soap, I use 4 Tablespoons of alkanet-infused olive oil as part of my total olive oil weight. This creates a light purple colored soap to highlight the delicate lavender scent. I know some who use more infused oil and some who use less to color their soaps, but 1-2 Tablespoons per pound of oil is a good rule of thumb to start experimenting with." - Alyssa

Note that the color of the soap mixture will look different during the mixing process than it will once cured. For instance, using alkanet-infused oil can make your soap mixture look grey in the soaping pot, but when the soap has cured, it becomes a lovely shade of lavender. Refer to the chart below for a listing of some of the herbs or botanicals that can be used to color your soap using this method.

Herb / Ingredient	Color
Activated charcoal powder	Black
Alkanet	Light pink to dark purple
Annatto seed	Yellow to orange
Calendula petals	Yellow to orange
Chickweed	Green
Cinnamon	Tan to brown
Cloves	Brown
Comfrey leaf	Light to dark green
Indigo	Dark blue
Kelp	Green
Madder root	Light pink to deep red
Nettle leaf	Bright green
Paprika	Peachy orange
Plantain	Green
Peppermint	Green
Pumpkin	Deep orange
Rosehip seed powder	Pink to tan
Spinach	Green
Spirulina	Blue green
Turmeric	Yellow gold
Woad	Light blue

Coloring Using Micas, Ultramarines and Oxides

There are many colorants available to the handcrafted soap maker. Adding colorants results in beautiful hues, but it is most important to add enough color to the soap without adding so much that it colors the lather, which can stain your skin or the shower.

To avoid wasted batches of soap, always test small amounts (follow manufacturer or supplier instructions) of colorants and then work your way up in subsequent batches of soap.

Always purchase soap-grade colorants from reputable manufacturers and suppliers. Ensure that the manufacturer or supplier states (in the case of natural colorants - oxides, for example) that all impurities have been filtered from the product.

Pigments - Some natural pigments exist, such as oxides, but most are manufactured in labs that imitate the chemical make-up of a natural product. Pigments are available in both powder and liquid form.

Oxides - A natural colorant obtained from iron oxides. Oxides are stable in cold process soap. Warning: a little oxide goes a long way. Follow manufacturer's instructions when using oxides in your formula.

Ultramarines - Most ultramarines are stable in cold process soap. Follow manufacturer's instructions when using ultramarines in your formula.

Other types of colorants

FD&C Colorants - FD&C is a classification of lab-created colorants approved for food, drugs, and cosmetics. FD&C colorants are mixed into a water base and can be used in a variety of soap types, including cold process soap (check your manufacturer or supplier instructions).

Micas - Micas are generally not stable in cold-processed soap. Most micas are naturally derived and are pearlescent, light reflecting ground powders. An advanced soap maker can use a tiny amount of mica between layers of cold-processed soap, or even in the soap overall, but this process takes a lot of experimenting and experience. Micas are usually used in cosmetics and melt and pour soap bases.

Resulting Color - Some fragrance and essential oils will affect the color of finished soap. For example, vanilla fragrance can tint a soap tan to dark brown, depending upon the percentage included in a soap formula. Lemongrass essential oil can tint soap a light yellow to deep golden color. Color that results from the chemical process (from fragrance and essential oils) often changes during the initial 2-3 days of curing. When you first remove a batch of uncured soap from the mold, do not be upset if the color isn't what you expected. Give the soap several days, even up to a week, to see what the true end result color will be.

Steps to add pigments

1. Follow the manufacturer's instructions. Some pigments disperse in water, others in oil or glycerin.

2. Remove a small amount (approximately 2 cups) of the soap mixture before it reaches trace and place it into a measuring cup or suitable small mixing container.

3. Mix the desired amount of pigment (usually ¼ teaspoon or less) with a small amount of water/oil/glycerin (approximately 2 Tablespoons) to ensure any clumps or streaks of colorant are broken up and evenly dispersed.

4. Add the mixed pigments to the small amount of soap in the measuring cup. Use a mixer or stick blender to ensure the colorant is evenly dispersed.

5. Add the colored soap mixture to the large soap mixture just before the large batch reaches trace, and before fragrance or essential oils are added.

6. Continue standard soap making procedures to finish your batch of soap.

Swirling Techniques

Next we'll describe four different ways to create swirls and designs in your soap. These are simple ways to incorporate multiple colors and make your soap more eye catching.

In the Pot Swirling

This method produces colorful wispy swirls in finished soap. The process involves removing portions of the soap mixture, adding colorants to the portions, and pouring the colored soap back into the mixing pot. The swirls are formed when the entire soap mixture is poured into the mold.

Additional Equipment Needed
Wooden skewer or similar thin utensil
Small container for colored soap mixture (one for each color)
Colorant(s)

Steps
1. Break down (premix) the colorants with water or oil (per manufacturer's instructions).

2. Add fragrance to the soap mixture before trace.

3. Bring the soap mixture to very light trace.

4. Pour ¼ to ½ of the soap mixture into smaller containers containing colorants. Hand stir the soap to distribute the color completely.

5. Gently hand stir the uncolored soap in the mixing pot to smooth it out. To avoid thickening the soap do not use a stick blender.

6. As if you have divided the uncolored soap in the pot into quarters of a clock, hold the small container(s) of colored soap above the mixing pot and pour about ¼-1/3 of the colored soap down into the middle of each of the four sections (at 3:00, 6:00, 9:00, and 12:00). Pour a small amount of colored soap into the middle of the pot.

7. Repeat step 4, pouring the same color of soap into each section, including the middle, leaving a small amount of colored soap in the container(s) to later drizzle on the top of the soap in the mold.

8. Insert a spatula into the middle of the first section of colored soap, holding it perpendicular to the mixing pot. While holding the spatula upright, drag it through the colored soap to the middle of the next colored soap section, and continue until you have returned to the starting point. At this point you have completed a full circle while dragging color to color. Without removing the spatula, drag through the soap in one diagonal line across the mixing pot, through the colored soap in the middle. Remove the spatula and do not stir.

9. Begin pouring the soap into one end of the mold. As the first end fills to the halfway point, continue to pour while slowly moving towards the opposite end of the mold. When the opposite end is nearly filled, continue pouring making an additional pass (pour) across the mold. Making two or three slowly poured passes helps the development of the swirls.

10. Gently tap the filled mold on the table top or work surface to settle the soap and remove any air pockets.

11. Drizzle thin lines of colored soap on the surface of the poured soap, from end to end of the mold. Using a skewer, pull the colored soap in diagonal lines from side to side of the mold. To form a beautiful swirl pattern on the top of the soap, use the skewer to pull the diagonal lines into a swirled pattern.

Tips

The soap must be kept at a thin trace throughout the swirling process to ensure it is not too thick for the final pour. Holding the soap mixture temperature down prior to trace will allow a longer time to color and pour the soap before it thickens. Thin trace normally occurs right after the soap mixture becomes opaque, just before it emulsifies.

Using softer oils, like olive, at 60% or more of the formula may help the mixture to remain thin while coloring and swirling.

Test fragrances before using the swirling method to ensure they do not accelerate or thicken trace, seize, or change the colors.

Test the colorants before using the swirling method to ensure they are the hue you desire, and to ensure they do not affect trace.

Premix the colorants, breaking them down with water or oil, to ensure the colorants are fully dissolved before mixing with soap. This eliminates clumping and leaves less time for the soap mixture to sit and thicken.

Clays, such as Rose Kaolin, can be added instead of colorants for the swirls. Premix the clay in water or oil to ensure it is fully dissolved, leaving no clumps in the colored soap.

Soap thickens as it cools. The in the pot swirling method necessitates moving at a smooth and steady pace from start to finish to ensure the mixture does not over thicken before the pours are completed.

When pouring soap into the small containers to be colored it helps to use a container that has measurement marks. For uniform colored portions, depending upon the overall size of the batch, many soap makers use 1 to 1 1/2 cups of soap per color. The determination of how much colored soap to add will depend upon the size of your entire batch of soap. You may need to make a few practice batches before you reach the amount of color you prefer.

Once the soap reaches light trace use a stick blender only in very short pulse increments. The more the soap is stirred, the thicker the soap becomes which inhibits the pour and the swirls from forming. We recommend hand stirring after light trace is reached to avoid over stirring.

If a whiter soap base is desired, you may add titanium dioxide pigment to the soap base during step 5.

Top Swirl

Adding a swirl of color to the top of a batch of soap is made easy by following a simplified version of the in the pot swirl method.

Additional Equipment Needed

Wooden skewer or similar utensil
Small container(s) for mixing colored soap
Colorant(s)

Steps

1. Break down the colorants with water or oil (per manufacturer's instructions).

2. Add fragrance to the soap mixture before trace.

3. Bring the soap mixture to a light trace.

4. Pour 1 to 1 ½ cups of soap into a small container and hand mix with colorant.

5. Hand stir the soap mixture in the pot, or stick blend at a pulse in short increments to avoid over stirring. Bring to medium trace.

6. Pour the soap into the mold.

7. From end to end of the mold, drizzle thin to pencil sized lines of the colored soap on the surface. Use a skewer to pull diagonal lines of the colored soap from side to side, then pull the diagonal lines into a swirled pattern.

Tips

The tips for In The Pot Swirling (see page 76) apply to top swirled soap. The amount of colored soap needed for the top swirl will vary based on how thick you want the colored layer, and how large the batch of soap is. For example, if you want a light swirl you may only want to color 1 to 1 ½ cups of soap. If you want a thick swirl with a ½ inch layer of colored soap on top, you may want to set 2 to 3 cups of soap aside for coloring.

Layering

Finished soap with multiple layers of contrasting color and scent is obtained through the layering process. In this section, each layer of soap is made in separate batches instead of dividing up one mixed batch.

Additional Equipment Needed

Colorants

Steps

1. Break down (premix) the colorants.

2. Divide the measurements of the soap formula in half and start standard soap making procedures for this halved batch.

3. Add color and fragrance to the soap mixture right before trace.

4. Mix until a thick but pourable trace is reached.

5. Pour into the mold.

6. Wait, approximately 5-10 minutes.

7. Mix a second batch of the halved recipe.

8. Add color and fragrance right before trace.

9. Mix until a thick but pourable trace is reached.

10. Pour into the mold, on top of the first layer.

Tips

To ensure the bottom layer sets up firm, which prevents the second layer from permeating the first, allow approximately 15 minutes (which includes steps 5-9) between pours.

Soap can be layered with more than two colors and scents. To do so, divide the original formula by the number of layers desired and repeat the layering steps until all of the pours are complete.

You may also embed soap between the layers. The newer the soap embeds are the softer they are, which leaves less chance of them popping out after the bars are cut. Add embeds after step 4 in a single layer (see steps on page 117 for embeds). Tap the mold on the counter or work table to release air pockets.

Double Pour

The double pour method is a process of pouring two colored soaps at once, or alternating between pouring several colors of soap into the mold, resulting in a marbled pattern. Double pour involves mixing one batch of soap, which is then divided in half and colored individually.

Additional Equipment Needed

Mixing bowls or containers for each color desired
Spatula, skewer, or similar tool to create swirls

Steps

1. Break down (premix) the colorants.

2. Mix the batch of soap.

3. Add fragrance prior to trace.

4. Bring soap to thin trace.

5. Pour soap mixture into two or more containers.

6. Color each container, hand stir only.

7. Pour a small portion of the first color of soap into the mold.

8. Pour a small portion of another color of soap into the mold.

9. Alternate between steps 7 and 8 until the mold is filled.

10. Insert a skewer or spatula down into the soap and pull through in zig zag motions from side to side of the mold. You may finish this off by pulling the skewer through the middle of the soap from end to end in one or two sweeps.

Tips

Temperature is important with the double pour process. The thicker the soap the more defined the color patterns are.

Double pour can also be obtained by pouring two colors simultaneously in step 7. Slowly pour each color at opposite ends of the mold until the mold is filled. Skip steps 8 and 9, and complete step 10 to create internal swirls or marbling if desired.

Once poured, avoid moving the mold to help the colors set and remain defined.

CHAPTER 8
SCENTING YOUR SOAP

There are two ways in which you can choose to scent your soap: with fragrance oils or essential oils. Fragrance oils are scents that have been created in a lab from a variety of aroma chemicals and essential oils. Many people are allergic to artificial fragrances. Fragrance manufacturers are expected to follow ingredient guidelines and to use ingredients that are within safety guidelines. However, companies are not required by the Food and Drug Administration (FDA) to release a listing of the exact chemicals that go into their fragrance oils, so there is no way of knowing if a fragrance oil contains a constituent that you are allergic to without using a product scented with that fragrance oil.

In contrast, essential oils are taken directly from a plant, fruit or herb, and have no added chemicals. They are pure, natural, and concentrated. Essential oils are used in aromatherapy, which is a centuries-old practice of using natural essences to promote mental and physical well-being. Essential oils are more expensive than fragrance oils, but may be worth the additional cost if you prefer an all-natural soap. Note that some individuals have reported allergies to essential oils. Next we'll discuss essential oils commonly used in soap. Fragrance families and notes will be discussed later in the chapter.

Essential Oils and Their Properties in Soap

Bay Laurel
INCI: *Lauris nobilis*
Label: Lauris nobilis (Bay Laurel) Leaf Oil
Fragrance Family: Spicy
Note: Middle
Sometimes referred to as laurel leaf oil, bay laurel oil is steam distilled from the leaves of the Bay Laurel tree. It has spicy and camphorous notes with sweet, fruity undertones. Bay laurel is often used in diffuser blends and is not used as often in soap making; however we included this oil to point out the differences between it and bay rum, with which it is often confused. Bay laurel can be irritating to skin and mucous membranes and should be avoided during pregnancy. Bay laurel blends well with bergamot, ginger, lavender, orange, frankincense, rosemary and patchouli.

Bay Rum
INCI: *Pimenta racemosa*
Label: Pimenta racemosa (Bay) Oil
Fragrance Family: Spicy
Note: Middle
Bay rum is steam distilled from the leaves of the Bay Rum tree or West Indies bay tree. Bay rum is considered a masculine scent with reviving, clearing, and antiseptic properties. It carries a spicy camphor-like aroma with a slight fruity, floral undertone. It is often used in aftershaves and hair tonics. It can be irritating to skin and mucous membranes and should be avoided during pregnancy. Bay rum blends well with lavender, rosemary, ylang ylang and clove.

Bergamot
INCI: *Citrus aurantium bergamia*
Label: Citrus aurantium bergamia (Bergamot) Fruit Oil
Fragrance Family: Citrus
Note: Top
Bergamot is a bright, sunny scent often used in aromatherapy to aid depression and anxiety. Tea drinkers may find the scent familiar, as bergamot is in Earl Gray tea blends. This reviving, soothing scent blends well with many other essential oils including other citruses and florals, ginger, rosemary and clary sage. The oil is cold pressed from the peel of the fruit, which is primarily found in Italy and France. Bergamot oil is phototoxic. (Note: Look for bergaptene-free bergamot oil that has been distilled to remove a portion of the phototoxic chemicals.)

Black Pepper
INCI: *Piper nigrum*
Label: Piper nigrum (Black Pepper) Seed Oil
Fragrance Family: Spicy
Note: Middle
Black pepper oil has anti-inflammatory properties and a warming effect, so it is frequently used in massage oils to help aching muscles and increase circulation. Black pepper oil also contains slightly aphrodisiac qualities. It is found in India and Madagascar where it is steam distilled from dried and crushed fruit. Black pepper blends well with other spices and florals, as well as rosemary, myrrh, tea tree and sandalwood.

Cedarwood

INCI: *Cedrus atlantica*
Label: Cedrus atlantica (Cedarwood) Bark Oil
Fragrance Family: Woody
Note: Base

Cedarwood holds a warm, woody aroma with sweet honey overtones. This masculine scent is reported to be fortifying and calming. Most noted for its 81 references in the Bible, cedarwood was one of the first essential oils used by the Egyptians for spiritual embalming purposes. Cedarwood is primarily found in India and steam distilled from wood chips of the tree. It blends well with other woody essential oils, black pepper, sweet orange, bergamot and patchouli. Cedarwood should be avoided during pregnancy.

Note that *Cedrus atlantica* is endangered. Other cedarwood variants include Texas cedarwood (*Juniperus Mexicana)* or Himalayan cedarwood (*Cedrus deodora*), both of which work well in soap.

Chamomile, German

INCI: *Matricaria recutita*
Label: Matricaria recutita (German Chamomile) Oil
Fragrance Family: Floral
Note: Middle

German chamomile, also known as blue chamomile, is a strong, fruity, herbaceous oil with a distinctive blue color. The sweet aroma is known in aromatherapy for soothing, calming, and balancing the body, so it is often recommended for those with tense nerves and high anxiety. German chamomile is steam distilled from the heads of the chamomile flower. It blends well with most other floral and citrus essential oils as well as petitgrain and patchouli. German chamomile should be avoided in early pregnancy.

Chamomile, Roman

INCI: *Anthemis nobilis*
Label: Anthemis nobilis (Roman Chamomile) Oil
Fragrance Family: Floral
Note: Middle

Roman chamomile is an herbaceous, sweet oil known for its soothing and relaxing properties. Tea lovers may be familiar with the scent because of its use in chamomile tea. It is found in the United Kingdom and the United States where it is steam distilled from the white flower. Roman chamomile blends well with most other florals and herb essential oils as well as bergamot and frankincense.

Clary Sage

INCI: *Salvia sclarea*
Label: Salvia sclarea (Clary Sage) Oil
Fragrance Family: Green
Note: Top
Clary sage is a radiant herbaceous oil with sweet undertones that is renowned as a "women's issues" remedy. Grown in the Kashmir Valley of India, also known as "Paradise on Earth", clary sage is steam distilled from flower buds. Clary sage's sweet, musky aroma often compliments citrus essential oils, lavender, cardamom, palmarosa, sandalwood, jasmine, and coriander. Clary sage should be avoided during pregnancy.

Clove

INCI: *Eugenia caryophyllus*
Label: Eugenia caryophyllus (Clove) Oil
Fragrance Family: Spicy
Note: Base
Clove is a warm and woody, yet slightly bitter, oil known for its warming effects. Clove was one of the first spices traded and can be dated back to 1721 BC in registries. It continued to be traded heavily throughout the 17th century until it became the most precious spice in the world. Primarily found in Madagascar and the Spice Islands, it is now produced globally where it is steam distilled from the flower buds and leaves. Clove can easily overpower a blend, so use in small amounts to blend with sweet orange, clary sage, lemon, and sandalwood. It is also known to accelerate trace. Clove oil should not be used during pregnancy.

Coriander

INCI: *Coriandrum sativum*
Label: Coriandrum sativum (Coriander) Seed Oil
Fragrance Family: Spicy
Note: Top
Coriander has a sweet aroma with herbaceous woody undertones and is known for its ability to relax and create clarity for creativity. Many people recognize coriander as the oil that comes from the same plant as cilantro, a common cooking ingredient that is from the leaf of the plant. It blends well with neroli, vanilla, bergamot, sandalwood, and clary sage. Coriander is primarily produced in Morocco, Romania, and Mexico. It is steam distilled from the plant seeds.

Eucalyptus
INCI: *Eucalyptus globulus*
Label: Eucalyptus globulus (Eucalyptus) Oil
Fragrance Family: Green
Note: Top
Eucalyptus is a stimulating, medicinal oil that has one of the most recognizable scents in aromatherapy. Its pungent, earthy fragrance clears the sinuses and stimulates the mind when steam inhaled, which makes it a common household staple during flu season. It is found in China, Spain, France, Madagascar, and Australia, where the plant leaf is steam distilled. Eucalyptus blends well with citrus or mint oils as well as lavender. *Eucalyptus globulus* is also the most well-known specie out of the 300 eucalyptus tree species.

Frankincense
INCI: *Boswellia carterii*
Label: Bosweillia carterii (Frankincense) Oil
Fragrance Family: Woody
Note: Base
Frankincense is a woody balsamic oil with a sweet fruity undertone that is most famous for being brought to the infant Jesus by the Three Wise Men. It is referenced in the Bible 24 times. Frankincense is found mainly in Somalia, Western India, Northeastern Africa, and Southern Saudia Arabia. It is steam distilled from the gum resin in tree bark. Frankincense blends well with florals, citruses, clary sage, basil and myrrh.

Geranium
INCI: *Pelargonium gravolens*
Label: Pelargonium graveolens (Geranium) Oil
Fragrance Family: Floral
Note: Middle
Geranium is a fresh rosy oil with a fruity undertone that is often used in aromatherapy blends for its balancing and uplifting properties. Because it is less expensive than rose and has a similar scent, geranium is often used in scent blends to extend a rose fragrance. Geranium is found in China, India, Morocco and Egypt, and is steam distilled from the plant's flowers, leaves and stalks. Geranium is a versatile essential oil, blending well with rose, lavender, black pepper, patchouli, lemon, neroli and rosemary. Note that geranium has been reported to accelerate trace.

Ginger

INCI: *Zingiber officinalis*
Label: Zingiber officinale (Ginger) Root Oil
Fragrance Family: Spicy
Note: Base

Ginger is a spicy, yet earthy, warming oil. Ginger's effect on the digestive system has made it a staple for those with nausea while traveling and for women during pregnancy. The oil is steam distilled from the rhizome of the plant, which is found in Sri Lanka, Indonesia, and Nigeria. Ginger can be overpowering in scent blends, so use in small amounts and blend with geranium, rose, frankincense, patchouli and ylang ylang. Ginger essential oil can irritate skin and is slightly phototoxic. It can also accelerate trace.

Grapefruit

INCI: *Citrus grandis*
Label: Citrus grandis (Grapefruit) Peel Oil
Fragrance Family: Citrus
Note: Top

Grapefruit is a tangy, refreshing and energizing oil with citrus top notes and floral undertones. Cold pressed from fresh fruit peels, grapefruit is found in the United States, Israel, and South Africa. It blends well with other citrus and spicy essential oils, as well as peppermint, rosemary, lavender and juniper. Grapefruit oil is phototoxic.

Jasmine

INCI: *Jasminum grandiflorum*
Label: Jasminum grandiflorum (Jasmine) Absolute
Fragrance Family: Floral
Note: Middle

Jasmine is a highly concentrated floral oil with a heady, exotic aroma. Jasmine is nicknamed "Queen of the Night", because that is when its perfume is strongest. It is harvested by hand at nighttime to collect the fragrant flowers, and the absolute is then solvent-extracted. Jasmine blends very well with citrus essential oils, along with rose, neroli, sandalwood and clary sage.

Lavender
INCI: *Lavandula angustifolia*
Label: Lavandula angustifolia (Lavender) Oil
Fragrance Family: Floral
Note: Middle

Lavender is best known for its calming, sedative properties (although using too much has the opposite effect – it stimulates, rather than calms). It was also the first essential oil that was proven to help heal burns. Lavender is steam distilled from the flowery tops of this perennial, bushy shrub, which is found in France, Hungary, Bulgaria, England and the United States. The sweet floral aroma blends well with most other essential oils, including lemon, peppermint and tea tree.

Lemon
INCI: *Citrus limonum*
Label: Citrus limonum (Lemon) Peel Oil
Fragrance Family: Citrus
Note: Top

Lemon is a bright, uplifting citrus scent with subtle, sweet undertones. It is one of the most easily recognized scents, as it is used in a variety of everyday products. Lemon oil is cold pressed from the peel of the ripe fruit, which is found in Argentina, Israel, Italy, and the United States. Lemon blends well with most essential oils, but especially florals and other citrus oils. Lemon, as most other citrus essentials, does not last long in soap, so we recommend 'anchoring' lemon essential oil with litsea cubeba or a tiny amount of patchouli oil to help the aroma stick. Lemon oil is phototoxic.

Lemongrass
INCI: *Cymbopogon flexuosos*
Label: Cymbopogon flexuosos (Lemongrass) Oil
Fragrance Family: Green
Note: Top

Lemongrass is a refreshing and uplifting oil. The fresh, herbaceous scent of lemongrass is commonly found in deodorants, detergents and insect repellants. It is primarily found in India and Nepal where it is steam distilled from fresh or partially dried grass. Lemongrass blends well with black pepper, ginger and rosemary in addition to most citrus and floral essential oils. Lemongrass may irritate skin.

Litsea Cubeba
INCI: *Litsea cubeba*
Label: Litsea cubeba (May Chang) Fruit Oil
Fragrance Family: Citrus
Note: Top
Litsea cubeba is a bright, lemony oil, which is also known as may chang or mountain pepper. Litsea cubeba is found in China, Japan and India where it is steam distilled from ripe fruits. It blends well with other citrus oils, as well as chamomile, clary sage, black pepper, tea tree, rosemary, eucalyptus and ylang ylang. In soap, litsea cubeba is also used as an anchor to help other citrus essential oils last longer in the finished bar of soap.

Mandarin
INCI: *Citrus nobilis*
Label: Citrus nobilis (Mandarin) Peel Oil
Fragrance Family: Citrus
Note: Top
Mandarin is the sweetest citrus oil and is renowned for being a well-documented essential oil that is safe for children and during pregnancy. Frequently used in Chinese medical practices, the name can be traced back to the Mandarins of China. It blends well with other citrus and spicy essential oils, in addition to lavender, juniper and petitgrain. Mandarin is cold pressed from fruit rinds and is found primarily in Brazil, Italy, Spain, and the United States.

Myrrh
INCI: *Commiphora myrrha*
Label: Commiphora myrrha (Myrrh) Oil
Fragrance Family: Woody
Note: Base
Myrrh is the oldest known essential oil, used by the Egyptians 4,000 years ago in religious ceremonies and for first aid. Today, people still enjoy its warm, spicy and earthy aroma. Myrrh is found in Ethiopia, Yemen and Somalia. It comes from resin released from cuts into the shrub's bark. The resin dries into "tears" and is then steam distilled to produce the thick, dark brown oil. Myrrh blends well with other resins, as well as lavender, patchouli, mandarin, sandalwood and rose. Myrrh should be avoided during pregnancy.

Neroli

INCI: *Citrus aurantium*

Label: Citrus aurantium (Neroli) Oil

Fragrance Family: Floral

Note: Top

Neroli, also called orange blossom is steam distilled from the flowers of the bitter orange tree. It has a gentle floral aroma with warm undertones. Neroli is found in Morocco, Spain, Italy, and Tunisia. Unlike many other citrus essential oils, neroli is <u>not</u> phototoxic. Neroli blends well with most other essential oils, but particularly well with frankincense, lavender and jasmine. Neroli tends to be quite expensive, so it is not commonly used in soap unless in very small amounts of a scent blend.

Palmarosa

INCI: *Cymbopogon martinii*

Label: Cymbopogon martini (Palmarosa) Oil

Fragrance Family: Floral

Note: Middle

Palmarosa is a delicate floral oil with sweet top notes and rose-geranium undertones. Palmarosa is primarily found in India where it is steam distilled from the fresh or dried grass. Palmarosa blends well with most other essential oils, including bergamot, clary sage, ginger, orange, clove, lemongrass, rosemary and frankincense.

Patchouli

INCI: *Pogostemon cablin*

Label: Pogostemon cablin (Patchouli) Oil

Fragrance Family: Earthy

Note: Base

Patchouli is a rich, warm and earthy oil typically associated with hippies from the 1960s, and is usually a scent one loves or hates. In reality, patchouli is excellent in a number of scent blends for soaping, as just a small amount helps to anchor citrus essential oils so the aroma sticks in finished soap. Patchouli thrives in tropical regions like Hawaii, Indonesia, Brazil, and Malaysia and is steam distilled from the leaf and flower portion of the plant. It is one of the few essential oils that actually improves with age. Patchouli blends well with orange, lavender, geranium, cedarwood, vetiver and ylang ylang.

Peppermint
INCI: *Mentha piperita*
Label: Mentha piperia (Peppermint) Oil
Fragrance Family: Green
Note: Top
Peppermint is a refreshing oil with antiseptic and astringent properties. Tea lovers may recognize this fresh minty aroma from peppermint herb tea. Peppermint is most commonly found in India, France, England, or the United States and is steam distilled from the flowering plant tops or leaves. It blends well with lavender, grapefruit, rosemary, eucalyptus and tea tree. The cooling effect of the menthol in peppermint may lead to a skin tingling sensation if too much peppermint oil is used in soap.

Petitgrain
INCI: *Citrus aurantium*
Label: Citrus aurantum (Petitgrain) Leaf Oil
Fragrance Family: Citrus
Note: Top
Petitgrain is a fresh woody oil with slight floral undertones. Though it is steam distilled from the same plant species as neroli and bitter orange, Petitgrain has a completely different aroma. Petitgrain is steam distilled from the leaves and sometimes twigs or branches while neroli is distilled from the blossoms and bitter orange is cold pressed from the fruit rinds. Petitgrain is found in Italy, France and Haiti. It blends well with most other floral and citrus essential oils in addition to black pepper, patchouli, clove, and clary sage.

Sandalwood
INCI: *Santalum album*
Label: Santalum album (Sandalwood) Wood Oil
Fragrance Family: Woody
Note: Base
Sandalwood is rich, woody and fragrant with floral undertones. Considered an aphrodisiac, both men and women are attracted to its aroma. Sandalwood is frequently used in high-end fragrances. It blends well with rose, lavender, black pepper, neroli, and bergamot. It is found throughout the Pacific and Eastern Indian Ocean regions where it is steam distilled from the interior bark of the tree or the roots.

Santalum album, or Indian sandalwood, is the most well-known and popular out of the sixteen sandalwood species. It is also endangered, so the Indian government regulates the availability of this essential oil. A suggested alternative is *Santalam spicatum,* or Australian sandalwood.

Sweet Orange

INCI: *Citrus sinensis*
Label: Citrus sinensis (Orange) Peel Oil
Fragrance Family: Citrus
Note: Top

Sweet orange is an inexpensive, sparkly citrus oil that has a variety of uses. Its fresh citrus scent and high content of limonene makes it popular in cleaning products. The joyful, familiar scent has given sweet orange the nickname of the "smiley oil". Sweet orange is cold pressed from the peel of the nearly ripe fruit. It is found in the United States, Brazil, and South Africa. It blends well with spice and other citrus essential oils along with patchouli, myrrh, sandalwood, geranium and clary sage. Sweet orange, like other citrus oils, tends to fade quickly in soap, so we recommend anchoring this with a bit of litsea cubeba or patchouli in your blend.

Tea Tree

INCI: *Melaleuca alternifolia*
Label: Melaleuca alternifolia (Tea Tree) Leaf Oil
Fragrance Family: Green
Note: Middle

Tea tree is a warm, earthy, medicinal oil with camphorous notes used for centuries for its antimicrobial properties. It is a popular ingredient in anti-acne products. Found in Australia, tea tree is steam distilled from the plant leaves and twigs. Tea tree is a scent that people tend to love or hate. It blends well with most spicy and green essential oils, along with peppermint, lemongrass, lavender and eucalyptus.

Thyme

INCI: *Thymus vulgaris*
Label: Thymus vulgaris (Thyme) Oil
Fragrance Family: Green
Note: Middle

Thyme is a herbaceous medicinal oil with sweet, spicy undertones. It has a strong herbal fragrance that may not appeal to everyone. Thyme is found in Spain, France, Germany and the United States where it is steam distilled from the plant flowers and leaves. It blends well with most other green essential oils, along with lemon, black pepper, pine and bergamot. Linalol thyme is the most gentle and non-toxic type of thyme oil. Thyme oil should be avoided during pregnancy.

Vanilla
INCI: *Vanilla planifolia*
Label: Vanilla planifolia (Vanilla) Bean Extract
Fragrance Family: Edible
Note: Base
Vanilla's sweet rich aroma is easily recognized as a soothing and comforting scent. It is a thick, dark brown oil that is solvent extracted from the vanilla bean or pod. Vanilla is often used a fixative in scent blends. Vanilla is found in Madagascar, Mexico and the United States. It blends well with bergamot, frankincense, jasmine, lavender, orange, rose, and ylang ylang.

Vetiver
INCI: *Andropogon zizanoides*
Label: Andropogon zizaniodes (Vetiver) Oil
Fragrance Family: Earthy
Note: Base
Vetiver is a smoky, herbaceous oil known as the "Oil of Tranquility". Its woody aroma is popular with both men and women. Vetiver is found in China, India, Malaysia, Sri Lanka and Indonesia where it is steam distilled from the roots. It blends well with ylang ylang, patchouli, orange, lavender, jasmine and geranium.

Ylang Ylang
INCI: *Cananga odorata*
Label: Cananga odorata (Ylang Ylang) Oil
Fragrance Family: Floral
Note: Base
Ylang ylang (pronounced "ilang-ilang") is a soothing, yet euphoric oil with a fresh floral and slightly fruity, exotic aroma. Ylang ylang is found in China, Madagascar and the Phillippines, and is steam distilled from the flower. There are different grades of ylang ylang produced, with ylang ylang-extra considered the most desirable. Ylang ylang extra is drawn off during the initial phase of distillation, and it has the most delicate, creamy aroma. Ylang II is next, and finally, ylang III is the last to be extracted. Ylang III has the most potent aroma. Regardless of the grade, ylang ylang blends well with most other floral and citrus oils, along with patchouli, clove and sandalwood. Note that ylang ylang has been reported to increase trace.

Take the time to research essential oils and learn how each can be used. For instance, lavender essential oil is used to calm and relax and promote deeper sleep. Some essential oils should not be used during pregnancy or with other health conditions. The following are some essential oils that are hazardous in any application and should NEVER be used:

Bitter almond	Cassia	Mugwort	Pennyroyal
Rue	Sassafras	Wintergreen	Wormwood

It is easy to make soap with a single note fragrance or essential oil: simply use the essential oil at .5 ounce per pound of soap oils in your formula. You'll need to experiment, as some oils may require more and some less to create the scent you're looking for. However, as we advance in our soaping techniques and experience, we want to create new scent blends, to add to our repertoire of available scents we can offer to our customers. But how do you blend scents to create something entirely new? First a brief lesson on the basics of scent blending.

Fragrance Families

Scents are typically categorized into sets of fragrance families. There are many versions of these categories out there, but for the purposes of this book, we'll use the following categories:

Citrus - Fresh, uplifting scents of citrus fruits, such as lemon, lime or bergamot.

Earthy - Deep, rich scents smelling of the earth, such as vetiver or patchouli.

Edible - Scents that are reminiscent of food, such as vanilla.

Floral - Flowers of all types, from the delicate neroli to lush rose or heady jasmine.

Green - This category encompasses fresh, leafy scents as well as more herbaceous or minty scents, such as rosemary, eucalyptus, lemongrass and thyme.

Spicy - Invigorating spices such as black pepper, cinnamon or clove.

Woody - Scents from wood or resinous material, including cedarwood, myrrh, and frankincense.

Notes

Fragrances are also classified by their notes:

Top - these usually evaporate quickly. They tend to be bright, light, fresh and uplifting. These are the first notes that one distinguishes in a blend, but top notes are often fleeting.

Middle - these notes provide the scent blend with body and balance the blend between the top and base notes. Middle notes can be more difficult to identify when first smelling a blend. They tend to be warm fragrances.

Base - these notes are heavy, and help to 'fix' the entire blend. Base notes tend to be rich and have an intense scent, which is why they are used in the smallest concentration in scent blends.

In general, oils in the same categories tend to blend well together. Here are some tips to help get you started with designing your own aromatic blends:

- Florals blend well with citrus, spicy and woody oils.

- Woody oils tend to blend well with all of the other categories.

- Spicy scents blend well with florals and citrus categories.

- Green scents blend well with citrus, woodsy and earthy scents.

It's also good to try to get at least one top note to lift the scent, a middle note to give body to the blend and a base note to ground the blend. But really, there's no limit to the blends that you can create. Just let your nose guide you. To start, try using the following formula:

30% top notes
50% middle notes
20% base notes

Place the drops of oil onto fragrance strips (writing down the number of drops you used so that you can easily recreate the blend if you love it). Use separate (labeled) fragrance strips for each oil. Then pick up all of the fragrance strips and wave them under your nose like a fan to see how they work together. Adjust the "formula" by adding or removing fragrance strips until you have a blend you think will work.

Next is the true test of the scent. Following your formula you've written down while using the fragrance strips, mix the scents into an amber glass bottle and close the lid. Shake to mix the oils and then leave the bottle to sit for a few days. This will allow the scents to blend together and you might find the overall aroma will change after the scents have had the chance to blend. After a few days have passed, return to the bottle and sniff to decide if you love or hate the blend. If you love it, then incorporate it into your creations. If you hate it, then start again.

Essential oils can sometimes be expensive or difficult to find. To broaden options or possibly help with cost, below is a list of common substitutions for essential oils with similar, though not exact results.

Essential Oil	Substitute Oil(s)
Lemon	Lime
Peppermint	Spearmint
Mandarin	Sweet Orange
Sandalwood	Equal parts Benzoin + Cedarwood
Rose	Geranium
Neroli	Ylang Ylang
Jasmine	Ylang Ylang
Melissa	Equal parts Petitgrain + Lemon
Vanilla Absolute	Benzoin
Patchouli	Vetiver
Tangerine	Orange
Cypress	Cedarwood
Clary Sage	Equal parts Sage + Nutmeg
Clove	Cinnamon

Scent blending is such a joy! Here are some simple blends:

Mojito	1 part peppermint to 3 parts lime
Patchouli Lavender	1 part patchouli to 3 parts lavender
Lemon Lavender	Equal parts lemon and lavender
Double Mint	Equal parts peppermint and spearmint
Exotic Calm	Equal parts sandalwood, frankincense and myrrh
Sweet & Spicy	Equal parts bay rum and sweet orange
Bright Citrus	2 parts litsea cubeba, 1 part each of sweet orange, lime and grapefruit
Uplifting Floral	3 parts ylang ylang, 2 parts bergamot and 1part petitgrain

*Note: a 'part' can be any unit of measurement that you select for your formula: milliliter, teaspoon, ounce, etc.

"I'm often asked 'What are the best essential oils to use in soap? Soap makers can easily spend a lot of money buying essential oils, so here's my top 10 picks (in alphabetical order) based on how they act in soap, how they smell and how easily they blend with other essential and fragrance oils." - Alyssa

Bergamot	Ginger
Lavender	Lemongrass
Lime	Litsea Cubeba
Patchouli	Peppermint
Spearmint	Sweet Orange

CHAPTER 9
ADDITIVES IN SOAP

One of the best benefits of handcrafting soap is adding ingredients to impart new textures, scents and features to the final product. Some of the more challenging ingredients used as additives include honey, clay and fruit and/or vegetable purees. Each of these additives along with exfoliants are discussed in this chapter.

Honey

Honey imparts a number of wonderful qualities to soap: it creates a moisturizing bar of soap, one that helps to attract and retain moisture in the skin; it naturally creates a light tan colored soap with a faint sweet scent, and its sugar content helps boost the lathering properties of soap.

Honey can be challenging to work with because the sugar content can rapidly increase the temperature of the soap mixture, which can lead to seizing or a volcano effect. It is critical to incorporate soap at low temperatures to help avoid these reactions from occurring.

We recommend using 1 Tablespoon of honey per pound of oils in your formula. For instance, if you are making a batch of soap that contains a total of 2 pounds of oils, then you would use 2 Tablespoons of honey.

Additional Equipment Needed

No additional equipment is needed to incorporate honey into your formula.

Steps

1. When measuring out the water portion of your formula, set aside some of the distilled water. We recommend setting aside an amount equal to the amount of honey you're using.

2. Warm this distilled water slightly.

3. Add the warmed distilled water to the honey and stir until well incorporated. This thins out the honey and will make it easier to incorporate into the soap mixture.

4. Set the honey and water mixture to the side.

5. Continue with standard soap making procedures.

6. When your soap has reached a very thin trace, slowly pour the honey/water mixture into the soap and stir well. Use a spatula to manually stir until it is completely mixed and both the color and texture of the soap are uniform.

7. Proceed with standard soap making procedures.

Tips

Be sure to keep soap temperatures low - around 100°F. The natural sugars in honey will increase the temperature of the soap, so it is important to keep the temperature of the soap mixture low so as to not encourage any of the problems mentioned earlier.

Honey can also increase trace, so be sure that your molds are ready to go before adding honey to the soap mixture.

Use a spatula to mix honey into the soap mixture. Using a stick blender will only speed up trace, and if the honey is not well incorporated before thick trace occurs, you will end up with globs of honey throughout the soap that can make the soap unsightly and difficult to use.

Do not add honey to the lye solution, as this can cause a very messy and dangerous volcano effect. It is better to add honey at a very light trace.

Some soap makers use up to 3% honey in their formula and will count the honey as part of the liquid in the formula. This means they will decrease the amount of distilled water used by 3%. For example, if a formula calls for 10 ounces of water, use 7 ounces of water and 3 ounces of honey (and simply add the honey at trace). The liquid portion of the formula remains the same 10 ounces, it is just a combination of water and honey.

Honey Soap Formula

Palm oil	5.52 ounces
Coconut oil	4.43 ounces
Pomace olive oil	4.43 ounces
Shea butter	2.23 ounces
Sodium hydroxide	2.18 ounces
Distilled water	5.21 ounces
Ground oatmeal	½ cup
Honey	2 Tablespoons

An Oatmeal, Milk and Honey fragrance would be nice scent to use here.

Clay

There are numerous types of clay, each with beneficial properties for a range of skin types. Below is a brief description of common types of clay, their color, benefits and how they're used in soap making. For each type of clay, we recommend a usage rate of 1 Tablespoon per pound of oils in your formula.

Bentonite

INCI: Bentonite
Label: Bentonite Clay Powder
Excellent at removing toxins from the skin, bentonite is often used in formulas for oily skin. This light gray clay is popular in shaving soap formulas to provide 'slip' or 'glide'.

French Green Clay

INCI: Montmorillonite
Label: Montmorillonite (French Green Clay)
Superb for drawing oils and toxins from the skin, this green clay is often used in soaps used for oily and acne prone skin. It can impart a natural green color to soap.

Rose Kaolin

INCI: Kaolinite
Label: Kaolinite (Rose Clay)
Excellent for normal to dry skin, this rose clay gently cleanses and exfoliates. It can impart a light pink color to soap.

Rhassoul

INCI: Moroccan Lava Clay
Label: Rhassoul (Moroccan Lava) Clay
Frequently used for detoxifying and gently exfoliating the skin, rhassoul clay can add a reddish brown color to soap.

White Kaolin

INCI: Kaolinite
Label: Kaolinite (White Clay)
The mildest of all clays, white kaolin is excellent for sensitive skin. This pure white clay gently exfoliates and cleanses, without drawing oils from the skin.

Additional Equipment Needed

No additional equipment is needed to incorporate clay into your formula.

Steps

1. When measuring the distilled water or oils for your soap formula, set aside a portion to be mixed with the clay. We recommend 1/8 cup of liquid or oil per tablespoon of clay. Some clay powders are drier than others, and you can add additional liquids or oils as needed to smooth out the mix.

2. In a small container, such as a quart mixing cup or bowl, add the liquid or oil to the clay and mix. We recommend hand mixing until the powdered clay is wet throughout. Ensure any clumps or remnants of dry clay powder are picked up from the bottom of your mixing container.

3. Mix with a stick blender until the clay dissolves into the liquid. The mixture should resemble a thin pudding, smooth, without clumps.

4. Set the clay mixture aside.

5. Follow standard soap making procedures. At thin trace, add the clay and mix with a stick blender. Ensure the clay is evenly distributed in the soap.

6. Pour into the mold.

Tips

Additional varieties of clay are available to soap making other than what are listed in this book. We've covered the most common and purest of clays. Some clays contain colorants that are not natural and may even include toxins. Pay close attention to the ingredients and INCI names when selecting clay to ensure the product does not contain unwanted additives.

Some clays are less gentle for sensitive and dry skin, and some should only be used once a week. When including clay in soap, research the usage recommendations provided by the product supplier. We recommend publishing a skin care warning or usage recommendations on your product label and on any corresponding documentation or website.

The formula for including clay in soap is generally 1 Tablespoon per pound of soap. Some clays thicken the soap at trace, so you may consider using less than 1 Tablespoon per pound of soap the first time you include clay.

Always mix clay with liquids or oil, working out any clumps before adding to the soap mixture.

Mix the clay prior to mixing the soap. By doing so, the clay mixture is ready to be added to the soap at a thin trace.

We do not recommend adding clay directly to the lye solution. Clay may thicken the soap mixture prematurely, giving a false trace. Adding clay to the end of the mixing process helps to preserve the properties of the clay.

Soap Formulas Using Clay

Goat Milk Facial Soap

This facial soap is wonderful for all skin types with the gentle cleansing properties of kaolin clay for normal to dry skin, and the soothing and healing properties of geranium rose and ylang ylang essential oils.

Palm oil	5.52 ounces
Coconut oil	4.43 ounces
Pomace olive oil	4.43 ounces
Shea butter	2.23 ounces
Sodium hydroxide	2.18 ounces
Distilled water	2.61 ounces
Goat milk	2.60 ounces
Rose kaolin clay	1 tablespoon
Geranium rose essential oil	.25 ounce
Ylang ylang essential oil	.15 ounce

Bay Rum Shaving Soap

This formula is especially nice if you use a chamomile and calendula-infused sunflower oil.

Coconut oil	4.80 ounces
Pomace olive oil	4.00 ounces
Palm oil	3.52 ounces
High oleic sunflower oil	1.60 ounces
Castor oil	1.28 ounces
Cocoa butter	0.80 ounces
Distilled water	4.80 ounces
Sodium hydroxide	2.29 ounces
Bentonite clay	1 Tablespoon
Bay rum essential oil	0.75 ounces

Palm Free Peppermint and Tea Tree Soap

This makes a nice deep cleansing facial bar.

Coconut oil	4 ounces
Shea butter	3.2 ounces
Pomace olive oil	2.4 ounces
Rice bran oil	2.4 ounces
Avocado oil	2.4 ounces
High oleic sunflower oil	0.8 ounces
Castor oil	0.8 ounces
Distilled water	3.56 ounces
Sodium hydroxide	2.18 ounces
French green clay	1 Tablespoon
Sodium lactate	1 Tablespoon
Peppermint essential oil	0.5 ounces
Tea tree essential oil	0.5 ounces

Fruit/Vegetable Purees

Purees are used for a number of reasons in soap. Some add color to the finished soap bar (although this color may fade over time). Purees can add a creamy appearance and texture to both the soap bar and the lather. Finally, there can be marketing appeal to using fruits and vegetables in your soap creations. Some common purees used in soap include:

Apple	Avocado	Banana	Berries
Carrot	Cucumber	Mango	Pear
Pineapple	Pumpkin	Tomato	Zucchini

Purees are simple to use and incorporate. If you don't want to puree the ingredient yourself, you can always buy pureed baby food to use in your formula. If you go this route, be sure to use Stage 1 food, for babies just beginning to eat, as this is the most pureed consistency. Also be sure that it is 100% carrots (or whatever you're using in your formula) and does not have any additional ingredients in it.

There is not a set recommended usage rate for using puree in soap, though we recommend keeping it to about 1/4 to 1/6 of the total amount of liquid needed. You should consider the puree as part of your water in the formula. For example, if it calls for 16 ounces of water and you have 4 ounces of puree that you want to use, then reduce your water by the 4 ounces. In this example, you would use 12 ounces of water and 4 ounces of puree.

Additional Equipment Needed

If you are going to puree the fruit or vegetable yourself, then you will need a blender or food processor with a 'puree' or 'grind' setting.

Steps

To puree the fruit or vegetable: Cook the desired amount of fruit or vegetable by steaming, microwaving or boiling.

1. Place the cooked fruit or vegetable and place it in a blender or food processor and cover with a lid.

2. Press the 'puree' or 'grind' button to mix the fruit or vegetable until it is a smooth, creamy consistency.

You can incorporate puree in one of two ways in your formula:

1. Add puree to the base oils and blend well before adding the lye solution.

OR

2. Add puree to the mix at light trace and blend well.

> "I have used both methods to incorporate puree into my soap formulas and haven't found one to be better than the other. Try both ways and determine which method works best for you." - Alyssa

Tips

Use a stick blender to incorporate the puree, regardless of which method you use to incorporate it into your formula. This will ensure that there are no blobs of puree in the formula and finished soap bars.

Remember to calculate the puree as part of your liquid in your formula. Otherwise, you will end up with a very soft bar of soap that will need to sit in the mold additional time before unmolding and will also take a longer time to cure.

Fruit and/or Vegetable Puree Soap Formulas

Pumpkin Spice Soap – All Natural Version

You'll notice that there isn't a water discount used in this formula, because the essential oils listed here can rapidly increase trace. So use the full water amount in addition to the puree to help keep the mixture fluid, and only bring the mixture to a <u>very</u> light trace before adding the essential oils.

Coconut oil	4.40 ounces
Pomace olive oil	4.00 ounces
Palm oil	4.00 ounces
High oleic sunflower oil	1.60 ounces
Shea butter	1.20 ounces
Castor oil	0.80 ounces
Distilled water	5.00 ounces
Sodium hydroxide	2.26 ounces
Pumpkin puree	1.25 ounces
Sweet orange (5-Fold) essential oil	0.50 ounces
Clove essential oil	0.10 ounces
Cinnamon essential oil	0.05 ounces
Nutmeg essential oil	0.05 ounces

Pumpkin Spice Soap – version #2

Coconut oil	4.40 ounces
Pomace olive oil	4.00 ounces
Palm oil	4.00 ounces
High oleic sunflower oil	1.60 ounces
Shea butter	1.20 ounces
Castor oil	0.80 ounces
Distilled water	4.10 ounces
Sodium hydroxide	2.26 ounces
Pumpkin puree	1.25 ounces
Pumpkin pie spice	½ teaspoon
Pumpkin scented fragrance oil	1.0 ounces

Exfoliants

Exfoliants provide extra scrubbing power and are used to remove dead skin cells. Start with a small amount of exfoliants and increase the amount in the formula as needed. Some options include:

- Pumice
- Poppy seeds
- Cornmeal
- Ground apricot kernels / walnut shells
- Ground oatmeal

Tips

When using exfoliating ingredients in soap, such as ground apricot kernels and pumice, they must be ground very finely, as close to a powder as possible, to avoid cuts and abrasions to the skin.

Add exfoliants to the soap mixture at trace.

CHAPTER 10
HARDENERS

Now we'll review ingredients that are used to harden your bars of soap. This chapter covers beeswax, salt, stearic acid and sodium lactate. No additional equipment is needed to incorporate any of these hardening ingredients in your formula.

Beeswax

Beeswax is made from worker honeybees, used to build honeycomb cells in their hives. It is a clear, waxy substance that hardens and turns a yellowish hue over time. Beeswax can be purchased in refined and unrefined versions and can be in blocks or pastilles (small, refined pellets). We recommend using pastilles, as they are easier to measure and melt compared to having to grate a block or chunk of beeswax.

Beeswax is used to create a harder soap bar. It is also reputed to help protect against soda ash or orange spots (see troubleshooting page 141). Using too much beeswax in your formula creates a sticky bar with decreased lather that drags across the skin, so keep it at around 1-2% of your total formula.

Beeswax can be saponified, so it needs to be added into your formula (not used as an additive) and run through a lye calculator. Also, beeswax has a higher melting point (around 145°F), so you'll need to soap at a warmer temperature to keep the beeswax in a liquid state while soaping.

When to Use Beeswax

Use beeswax when you want to incorporate your hardener at the same time you're melting and heating your solid and liquid oils in your formula. Natural (unrefined) beeswax may impart a slight honey scent to the finished bar of soap.

Steps

1. Melt the beeswax in your soaping pot over low to medium heat.

2. Once melted, add the other liquid and solid oils to the soaping pot and stir gently to blend.

3. Continue with standard soap making procedures.

Tips

If you're concerned about the beeswax inhibiting lather, you may want to include castor oil in your formula, which will help boost the lather in the finished soap bar.

Beeswax can accelerate trace, so be prepared to work quickly and have all of your molds prepared in advance.

If you're making vegan soap (one with no animal products or byproducts), candelilla wax or carnauba wax can be used in your formula. Candelilla and carnauba are harder than beeswax, so you'll need to use less of these waxes in your formula to ensure your bar of soap isn't too brittle. You will need to experiment with your formula if using vegan waxes.

Salt

Using salt in your formula as a hardening agent is different than creating a salt bar, which we discuss in Chapter 11. The type of salt used for hardening your soap is standard table salt, and it is very easy to incorporate into your formula. Use ½ teaspoon (tsp) of non-iodized salt per pound of oils in your formula. You will likely be able to unmold your soap loaf faster and easier than you normally would simply by adding a bit of salt to your formula.

When to Use Salt

Use salt in your formula when you want an easy and inexpensive additive to help harden your soap loaf.

Steps

1. Measure out the amount of salt needed for your formula.

2. Add salt to your water and mix well until the salt is fully dissolved.

3. Add lye to salt water solution.

4. Proceed with standard soap making procedures.

> "I have found that using salt creates a harder soap initially, which lets me unmold and cut the bars sooner than I would otherwise, but I have not noticed a difference in the finished soaps after a standard cure time." - Alyssa

Stearic Acid

Stearic acid is one of the most common saturated fatty acids found in nature. It can be found in both animal and vegetable fats and oils. If you want to avoid animal products, then be sure to use vegetable-based stearic acid. In soap, stearic acid is used to harden the bar of soap and enable you to unmold the bar earlier. Stearic acid contributes to a creamier bar of soap. It does decrease bubbles a bit, though. It is also reputed to create bars that last longer in the shower due to their hardness.

Stearic acid has its own saponification value, so it must be calculated as part of your oils. Use about .5 ounces per pound of oils in your formula. Stearic acid has a high melting point of 157° F.

When to Use Stearic Acid

Use stearic acid when you want an inexpensive, odorless and easy-to-use method of hardening your soap bars.

Steps

1. Melt the stearic acid in your soaping pot along with the other hard oils.

2. Once melted, add the liquid oils to the soaping pot and stir gently to blend.

3. Continue with standard soap making procedures.

Tips

Heat the oils at a higher temperature to ensure all of the stearic acid has fully melted before mixing with the lye solution. Otherwise, you may find white specks of unmelted stearic acid throughout your soap.

Stearic acid can speed up trace, so be sure to have all of your molds ready to go before starting the soap making process.

If your formula already has a high amount of hard oils such as coconut, cocoa butter or palm kernel oil, then you may want to avoid using stearic acid. Using stearic acid in a high hard-oil formula will lead to cracking, and brittle bars.

Sodium Lactate

Sodium lactate is a clear liquid salt that comes from the natural fermentation of sugars found in beets and corn. It is a natural humectant and pH balancer. Sodium lactate is used, among other applications, to produce a harder bar of soap that lasts longer in the shower. Some say that using sodium lactate helps to prevent cracking. It is easy to incorporate into soap formulas and has no odor. We recommend using 1 teaspoon per pound of oils.

When to Use Sodium Lactate

Use sodium lactate when you want an easy way to harden your soap without having to melt a solid product, like stearic acid or beeswax.

Steps

There is no need to change any of the oils, lye or liquid amounts when using sodium lactate. You can add Sodium lactate to your formula in a number of ways. Experiment to see which method works best for you.

To water

1. Measure the sodium lactate portion of your formula and set aside.

2. Measure the water portion of your formula.

3. Pour the sodium lactate into the water and mix well.

4. Continue with standard soap making procedures.

To cooled lye water

1. Measure the lye portion of your formula and set aside.

2. Measure the water portion of your formula.

3. Slowly pour the lye into the water and stir, taking care to follow safety precautions. Mix well and set lye solution aside to cool.

4. Measure the sodium lactate portion of your formula and set aside.

5. Once the lye solution has cooled, slowly pour the sodium lactate into the lye solution and gently stir to mix.

6. Continue with standard soap making procedures.

To soap mixture

1. Following standard soap making procedures and safety precautions, create a lye solution and set aside to cool.

2. Melt hard and soft oils.

3. Measure the sodium lactate portion of your formula and set aside.

4. Add the lye solution to the melted oils and stir gently with a soaping spoon or spatula (not with a stick blender). Stir only long enough to barely blend the mixture.

5. Add the sodium lactate to the soap mixture before trace occurs. Gently mix with a stick blender to fully incorporate the sodium lactate into the soap mixture.

6. Continue with standard soap making procedures.

Tips

Do not use a heavy water discount when using sodium lactate.

Standard usage rates are 1-3% of the total formula. However, using too much sodium lactate may result in a crumbly bar of soap, so start with 1% first and then decide if you need to bump it up for future batches.

"I like to use sodium lactate in my formulas that have higher percentages of soft oils, as it does create a harder bar of soap. I prefer to add sodium lactate to my water before adding lye, but have never had an issue when incorporating it at other times during the soap making process."- Alyssa

Formula Using Hardeners

<u>The Bee's Knees Soap Bar</u>

This formula has a higher amount of water compared to most formulas in this book due to the likelihood of the beeswax and honey increasing trace. It may take longer to harden and cure, but will become a lovely bar of soap. Leave unscented, or use a honey fragrance oil that does not accelerate trace. Adding ground oatmeal is nice too!

Pomace olive oil	7.20 ounces
Coconut oil	4.00 ounces
Palm oil	3.20 ounces
Beeswax	0.80 ounces
Castor oil	0.80 ounces
Honey	1 Tablespoon
Distilled water	5.76 ounces
Sodium hydroxide	2.19 ounces

CHAPTER 11
SALT BARS

Salt bars are created from soap formulas that contain a high percentage of salt. Salt in soap bars assists with cleansing, boosting lather, hardening of the bar, exfoliation and detoxifying of the skin.

Use sea salt or kosher salt in salt bars. Do not use iodized salt, as it will discolor the soap. Do not use Dead Sea salt, as it contains too many minerals and will cause the soap to sweat. Epsom salt will also lead to sweating if used in salt bars.

Additional Equipment Needed
No additional equipment is needed to make salt bars.

Steps
1. Select a cold process soap formula containing a high percentage of lathering oil, such as coconut oil. Salt decreases the ability of soap to bubble; however, the salt will help develop a creamy thick lather. Some soap makers superfat salt soap at 15-20% to offset the drying effects of coconut (or other high lathering oils).

2. Measure salt, matching salt amount up to 100% of the oils in the formula. Note: you can use 50-70% salt, for example: with 100 ounces of oils in a formula, you would use 50 – 70 ounces of salt.

3. Follow the cold process soap making instructions from pages 19-20. Bring to a medium trace.

4. Pour the salt into the soap mixture and hand stir. Salt accelerates trace. Note: hand stir immediately, as quickly as possible, to ensure the soap does not over-thicken before it is poured into the mold.

5. Monitor the soap closely. It will harden quickly, so cut the bars within 2-4 hours (or as soon as it is hard enough to cut).

Tips
Do not use fragrances or other ingredients that are known to seize or accelerate trace in salt soap, otherwise, most cold process formulas accommodate the addition of salt.

To prevent sweating, cure and store salt bars in a very dry area, preferably an area with low humidity.

Do not wait too long to cut salt bars, or they will crumble.

CHAPTER 12
EMBEDDING

Embedding consists of inserting solid finished pieces of soap into a fluid soap mixture.

Cold process soap is not transparent, meaning you cannot see all of the layers of embeds inside the soap unless it is cut. However, embedding shapes and chunks of soap can create a gorgeous confetti, stained glass, or multi-colored appearance.

We are focused on cold process soap instruction in this book. However, you can embed translucent melt and pour soap pieces into cold process soap, and you can also embed cold process soap into melt and pour soap.

Steps

1. Cut soap to be embedded into chunks or pieces.

2. Follow the cold process soap making instructions on pages 19-21. Note: Trace should be thick enough to allow embeds to remain inside the soap mixture, but not thin enough to allow the embeds to sink to the bottom.

3. Layer #1 - Pour the thickened soap to the desired first layer height in the mold.

4. Place the embeds on top of the layer.

5. Using a spatula or gloved hands, gently press the embeds to release air pockets.

6. Layer #2 - Pour soap mixture over embeds to desired layer height.

7. Repeat steps #3, 4 and 5, and repeat as many times as desired until mold is filled with soap.

8. Continue with standard soap making procedures.

Tips

Soap used for embeds should be as new as possible, meaning, the softer the soap (not fully hardened) the better it will stick inside the bars when cut or used.

When using older fully hardened soap as embeds cut the soap to chunks or shapes that are small. This helps the embeds stick to the newly poured soap as it heats during the gel phase.

Instead of layering embeds, you can stir very small pieces of embeds into the soap mixture before it is poured. To release air pockets, gently tap the filled soap mold several times on the table or work surface.

When layering embeds, instead of bringing the entire batch of soap to trace before pouring, you can divide it up before it reaches trace. For example: mix the batch until thoroughly combined. Separate into 2 or 3 containers. Mix container 1 until trace, pour into mold, and add embeds. Mix container 2 until trace, pour into mold, add embeds, and repeat for a 3rd layer if desired.

"Embeds are a great way to creatively use colorful or fragranced soap that did not turn out how you had planned. I once made soap that looked and smelled like dark chocolate. It was gorgeous, however, it produced an undesirable dark tan lather. I broke the soap into chunks and embedded it into minty scented light green soap. The scent and appearance was beautiful, and the lather problem was perfectly resolved." - Mary

Confetti Soap

Instead of embeds, add small pieces of colorful soap to the batch to create a colorful confetti look to finished soap.

Steps

1. Cut soap to be embedded into small chunks or pieces or use a grater or potato peeler to cut soap 'curls'.

2. Follow standard soap making procedures from pages 19-21. Note: Trace should be a medium trace, allowing the soap pieces to be stirred evenly into the mixture, but not so thin that the pieces sink to the bottom of the mixture or mold.

3. Stir the soap pieces into the soap mixture.

4. Pour the soap into the mold.

5. Tap the mold onto the work surface to remove air pockets.

6. Continue with standard soap making procedures.

CHAPTER 13
REBATCHING

Rebatching is a method used for correcting or adding additional properties to finished soap. French-milled and hand-milled are also terms for rebatching when the process adds additional nutritive, fragrance, or other value to the soap.

Benefits of rebatching include:
- Preserve scent
- Preserve properties of essential oil
- Preserve properties of herbs or other soap additives
- Preserve properties of colorants
- Correct a failed batch

Additional Equipment Needed
Grater
Double boiler
Soap (pre-made cold or hot process)
Liquid (distilled water)
Essential oils, fragrance, colorant, or additives of choice
Soap mold

Steps
1. Grate the soap.

2. Weigh out 2 or 3 ounces of liquid per pound of soap (enough to add moisture to the soap).

3. Add liquids to soap.

4. Place soap in top of double boiler and gently heat until melted, stirring constantly to blend the soap and liquids.

5. Once the soap has melted, add additional ingredients (colorants, fragrance, herbs, etc.)

6. Press the soap into mold, gently tap mold onto hard surface to remove air pockets.

7. Continue with standard soap making procedures.

Tips

Do not rebatch soap if it is not safe for use such as soap with lye pockets, see Troubleshooting, Chapter 16).

Fresh cold process soap about 5-7 days old is best for rebatching. The liquids in the soap have not fully evaporated, making it less prone to seizing or scorching. Older soap has a lower moisture content and may require more liquids when melting.

The soap will scorch if it is too dry while melting. Continue to add liquids in very small amounts throughout the melting process to keep it moist. Keep in mind that if too much liquid is added, the soap will take much longer to cure.

Use low temperatures when melting soap. Applying high heat can lead to scorching.

The melted soap will take on a translucent appearance and will resemble a very thick pudding when it is ready for the mold.

Smaller molds that hold individual bars of soap are preferred for rebatching. Individual molds allow the soap to be hand-pressed into smaller compartments, which promotes a smoother appearance by lessening the chance of hidden air pockets.

Always wear gloves and protective eyewear while rebatching. Newer soap may be caustic, and hot soap can burn skin.

Alternate Methods

The soap and liquids may be placed in a heat proof, baking, or other type of oven proof bag. Place the sealed bag in the top of the double boiler in water. Massage or squish the mixture in the bag with gloved hands as it melts. Use low heat to ensure the soap does not overheat. While carefully handling the bag, pour the melted soap into the mold.

The soap and liquids may also be melted in a crock pot on low heat setting. The process must be monitored to ensure the soap does not dry out or scorch. Stir frequently. Ladle melted soap into the mold.

"Patience and practice are key when learning the rebatching process.

Rebatched soap can appear mottled or rustic. Of course, this could be just the look you want!

I once grated and combined two fragranced soaps that were not scented as I preferred. The rebatched combination of fragrances made a unique and beautifully scented soap.

I also ruined a perfectly good food processor by grating soap. I find the best grater for soap to be the old-fashioned metal hand grater commonly used for grating cheese and vegetables." - Mary

CHAPTER 14
CALCULATING YOUR OWN SOAP FORMULA

After a soap maker has successfully made a few batches of soap, they often get the itch to experiment and create their own formulas. After all, this is part of the fun and adventure of handcrafting soap - dreaming of new ingredient combinations and discovering how they turn out in soap. And isn't it one of the reasons you picked up this book - to try new things?

But how do you know which oils to use and how much of each to include in your formula? Most soap makers base the percentages used of each ingredient on the hardness, conditioning, and lathering properties that each will give to the finished soap. We went into great detail about soap making oils in Chapter 3. After the oils are selected how then do you determine much liquid and lye are needed? There are two ways in which you can calculate your own soap formula: by using an online lye calculator, or calculating it by hand. This chapter will review each method, and you'll be ready to start creating your own formula in no time!

Online Lye Calculators

The technology of today's world allows us to quickly and easily create and adjust soap formulas with just a few clicks on your keyboard. An online lye calculator will take the information you enter and calculate the exact amounts of each ingredient needed to make the soap formula in the size mold you're using.

There are a number of online lye calculators available, and we've included links to some in Appendix 1. Each is slightly different but most generally work in the same manner, and all have help buttons to define terminology or further clarify each step.

Steps

1. Enter the type of lye in your formula. Remember that for bar soap, you use sodium hydroxide: NaOH.

2. Enter the total volume of the mold. (Refer to page 128 in this chapter on how to calculate this for new molds).

3. Enter your preferred unit of measurement - grams, ounces or pounds.

4. Enter the percent of water in the formula - either as a percentage of the oils (some online calculators have set this to default to 38%, but you can edit this with a water discount, which was discussed in Chapter 2) a percentage of lye concentration or a water to lye ratio.

5. Enter the amount of superfat you want in your formula. Some online calculators default to 5%, but you can move this amount up or down.

6. Enter each of the oils in your formula, either by weight or by percentage of the total formula.

7. Click 'Calculate'.

The online calculator will then generate information that can be printed as a document or saved to your computer (note: the save feature is not available on all online lye calculators). It will tell you the exact amounts of each ingredient needed to create that particular formula. It also has a section for you to take notes regarding additives, time it takes to trace, etc. so that you'll be able to recall at a glance how this specific formula worked for you.

Calculating Formulas By Hand

Some prefer to calculate formulas 'the old school' way - by hand. This too, generates the same results (determining how much liquid and lye to use in your formula) but may take a little longer than using an automated lye calculator. Neither method is better, and we include both in this book so you can choose which works best for you.

To calculate a formula by hand, follow these steps. (A detailed example is written out below for you to follow as well):

1. Select the oils and butters that you will include in your formula.

2. Determine the amount of each oil/butter that you will use. Refer to Determining the Volume of a Mold on page 128 if you're not sure what the total weight of oils should be.

3. Calculate how much lye is required to saponify your soap:
   - Amount (weight) of oil multiplied by its SAP value = total weight of lye needed to saponify that specific oil. (See Chapter 3 for oil SAP values.)

4. Add up each lye value for each oil to determine the total amount of lye needed for the formula.

5. Calculate the amount of water required for your formula:
   - Total weight of oils multiplied by .3 = total weight of water

Here is an example of a calculation written out:
1. You have chosen a formula that includes 40.8 ounces:
   39% of the formula: olive oil (15.9 ounces)
   20% of the formula: coconut oil (8.16 ounces)
   20% of the formula: palm oil (8.16 ounces)
   12% of the formula: avocado oil (4.90 ounces)
   9% of the formula: shea butter (3.68 ounces)

2. Each oil has an SAP value (multiply the SAP value by the total ounces to determine the amount of lye needed to saponify each oil):
   15.9 ounces olive oil x (SAP value .133) = amount of lye 2.11
   8.16 ounces coconut oil x (SAP value .180) = amount of lye 1.47
   8.16 ounces palm oil x (SAP value .139) = amount of lye 1.13
   4.90 ounces avocado butter x (SAP value .132) = amount of lye .65
   3.68 ounces shea butter x (SAP value .126) = amount of lye .46

3. Add up the amount of lye for each oil to determine the total amount of lye needed for the formula:
   2.11 + 1.47 + 1.13 + .65 + .46 = 5.82 ounces

4. Calculate the amount of water needed for the formula (total weight of oils multiplied by .3):
   40.8 ounces x .3 = 12.24 ounces

Sample Formula Moisturizing Bar

Olive oil	15.9 ounces
Coconut oil	8.16 ounces
Palm oil	8.16 ounces
Avocado butter	4.90 ounces
Shea butter	3.68 ounces
Sodium hydroxide	5.82 ounces
Water	12.24 ounces

Determining the Volume of a Soap Mold

Now that we've discussed how to calculate a soap formula, this is the method for calculating the volume of soap that a mold will hold.

Measure the inside of the mold as follows:

1. Multiply the length by the width by the height (L x W x H) to determine the total volume.

2. Multiply the total volume by .40 to calculate the ounces of oils required.

Example:
1. Measure the inside of the mold, in this example the measurements are length 17", width 3", height 2"

2. Multiply 17 x 3 x 2 to determine the total volume = 102

3. Multiply the total volume 102 x .40 = 40.8 ounces of oils required in the formula.

(The mold will hold 40.8 ounces of oils plus any water and lye that the soap formula contains. The calculation above automatically allots for the water and the lye.)

Sizing the Volume of a Soap Formula to a Mold

Now that we've calculated the size of a mold, this is the formula for sizing the volume of a soap formula to a mold.

In this example the mold requires 40.8 ounces of oils. Before recalculating, the soap formula contained 24 ounces of oils.

1. Since the mold requires 40.8 ounces, divide 40.8 ounces by 24 ounces = 1.70

2. Multiply each oil in the formula by 1.70

9.35 ounces olive oil x 1.70 = 15.9
4.80 ounces coconut oil x 1.70 = 8.16
4.80 ounces palm oil x 1.70 = 8.16
2.88 ounces avocado butter x 1.70 = 4.90
2.17 ounces shea butter x 1.70 = 3.68

Re-calculate the water and lye according to your new formula. You may use math (in this example 1.70 x the lye or the water) or, for more accurate measurements you can run the oils through a soap calculator, which is discussed on page 125.

In this example we'll convert the measurements of the water and lye from the formula requiring 24 ounces of oils to the formula containing 40.8 ounces of oils:

      3.42 ounces lye x 1.70 = 5.82
      7.21 ounces lye x 1.70 = 12.24

Tip:
Occasionally, you may need to bump up a final calculation of an oil, for example: from 3.67 to 3.68 ounces, to ensure the total volume of oils equals the amount needed in the formula (as in the example of the formula on page 128).

CHAPTER 15
FINISHING TOUCHES

Now that we've discussed the ins and outs of advanced methods of soap making, we'll talk about the beautiful and unique ways you can add a personal touch to finished bars of soaps. The possibilities are endless but we'll talk about beveling, stamping, using a serrated soap cutter, and adding waves to the top of the soap bar.

Top of Soap Waves

Waves and peaks can be added to the top of a bar of soap using remnants of the soap mixture.

Additional Equipment Needed

Spatula
Skewer

Steps

1. Pour the soap mixture into the mold. Leave a small amount in the soap pot.

2. Using a spatula, scrape small amounts of soap from the soap pot. Plop the soap randomly on top of the soap in the mold. If the soap is thin enough to do so, you can also use the spatula to drop lines of soap from end to end of the mold.

3. If the soap mixture is thin enough, use a skewer to lightly swirl the soap into a waved or peaked design.

4. Cover and insulate the soap if necessary.

Tips

If the soap needs to be insulated, cover the mold with an upside down plastic shoe box, or a cardboard box lined in plastic, and insulate the outside of the box. This prevents the design of the soap from being flattened.

Dusting

Dusting the top of finished soap, especially when the soap has waves or peaks, gives your soap additional color appeal and sheen.

Additional Equipment Needed

Mica or Glitter Dust (very fine, skin grade)
Paint Brush
Sifter

Steps

1. After adding waves or peaks to the top of the soap in the mold use a sifter, or sprinkle by hand the mica or glitter dust lightly over the soap.

Tips

If the soap is thick enough, use a soft paint brush to brush the dust or mica on the soap.

If the soap needs to be insulated, cover the mold with an upside down plastic shoe box, or a cardboard box lined in plastic, and insulate the outside of the box. This prevent the design of the soap from being flattened.

Beveling

Beveling involves taking the outer edge off of a finished bar of soap, giving it a polished appeal. Beveling helps to remove jagged or broken edges.

Additional Equipment Needed

Vegetable peeler or handheld beveler

Steps

1. Gently run the peeler or beveler along the outer edges of the soap bar to remove a minimal amount until you obtain the edge that you desire.

Tips

Allow the soap to partially cure before beveling. The soap should be hard enough to allow beveling but not so hard that the soap cracks or becomes damaged by the process. Depending upon the formula, many soap bars are ready for beveling between 1 to 2 weeks.

Save the scraps from the beveling process. Store in a sealed container or zip lock plastic bag. Use the scraps to make confetti rebatched soap.

Wavy Edge Cutting

Hand cutters are available with wavy serrated edges, which produces a cut bar with a serrated edge rather than a smooth straight edge.

Additional Equipment Needed

Hand Held Cutter or Soap Slicer with wavy edge

Steps

1. Use the wavy edge slicer or soap cutter as you would any soap slicer to cut the bar of soap. Cut with the wavy edge on either the top or long side of the bar.

Tips

Cut the soap bar when it is firm enough to hold the wavy shape, but not so hard that the soap cracks between the wavy edges.

Stamps

Soap stamps are a way to add a unique or personalized touch to finished bars.

Additional Equipment Needed

Soap Stamp

Steps

1. Center the stamp on the bar of soap.

2. Lightly tap or press the stamp into the bar.

Tips

Allow the soap to harden for 8 to 12 hours after cutting, or allow it to harden longer for formulas using a high percentage of soft oils. This helps the stamp to press into the soap without lifting soap up out of the bar when stamped.

Residue in the soap stamp will make the impression less clear. Ensure the stamp is kept clear of soap remnants.

CHAPTER 16
TROUBLESHOOTING

Even after many years of soap making experience, imperfections in soap or problems are going to occur. The best preventative tools include following precise formulas, setting time aside for soap making, patience and taking detailed notes to determine which ingredient(s) tend to cause problems. This section is a compilation of the most common soap making problems, how to recognize them and how to avoid them.

Signs of Trouble in the Soap Pot

Problem: Eruption (Volcano Effect)

Eruption quickly occurs without advanced warning, and is a very dangerous problem. The soap mixture bubbles up, rapidly grows in size, and erupts into the air or over the sides of the mixing pan. Soap eruptions can happen when the oils are too hot for the lye mixture to be added. The stirring of the soap mixture further increases the temperature. The addition of fragrance oils and additives that contain sugar can also increase the already too hot mixture. Eruptions can also occur after overheated soap is poured into the mold.

How to Avoid/Protect Yourself
Check ingredient temperatures *before* mixing.

Always cover work surfaces with protective materials like newspaper or plastic.

Always wear gloves, long sleeves, and safety glasses.

Keep vinegar in the soap making areas at all times. Vinegar can help neutralize caustic soap materials and burns on the skin.

Problem: Seizing

Soap mixture thickens very rapidly to the point it can no longer be poured.

How to Avoid

Check the ingredient temperatures before mixing. Some fragrance and essential oils are sensitive to heat. Always allow the ingredients to cool to the desired temperature before combining and mixing.

Some fragrance or essential oils promote seizing. Always add the fragrance or essential oils at the very end of the mixing process, immediately before the mixture is poured into the soap mold.

When seizing does occur in the soap pot, the soap is not lost. While wearing heavy rubber gloves, spoon the mixture into the mold. Press the seized mixture into the mold with a spoon, spatula or your well-gloved hands. After pressing the soap into the mold, cover, and allow the soap to set; continue with standard procedures from this point forward.

> "Despite our best attempts, some fragrances cause a batch of soap to seize. The decision has to be made whether to use the fragrance again. With a few of my most popular scents I've learned to expect the soap to seize. I press the seized soap mixture into the mold, carefully, with gloved hands. I present the finished soaps to my customers with the beautiful handcrafted and "rustic" look that results." - Mary

Problem: Mixture Will Not Trace

Sometimes the soap mixture will not trace during the mixing process.

How to Avoid

Some butters and oils will lengthen the time it takes to bring the mixture to trace; an example would be soap that is very high in coconut or olive oil.

The formula may have been measured incorrectly.

If too much liquid and not enough lye is used, the soap may never reach trace, and may need to be discarded.

How do you know when to give up on your attempt to bring soap to trace? When using a stick blender at a steady speed, trace should occur within 15-30 minutes or less. Hand stirring may take hours before trace is reached.

Problem: Mixture Separating

This is when the soap appears to form lumps while mixing.

How to Avoid

Quick action is necessary.

Some fragrance, essential oils, and pigments or colorants will cause streaking in the soap mixture before they have completely mixed in, which leaves the appearance of separation of ingredients. Continue stirring.

Dry ingredients, such as ground oatmeal, may sink to the bottom of the mixture if they are not stirred in properly. Continue mixing to break up the additives. It is always best to ensure that dry materials are not clumped or packed before adding to the soap mixture. Only add the ingredients right before the mixture reaches trace.

Problem: Lumpy Mixture

This is when the soap appears to form lumps while mixing.

How to Avoid

Quick action is necessary, as lumping most often occurs when the soap mixture is preparing to seize. Lumping may also occur at trace when a short amount of mixing is still needed.

As soon as you see the formation of lumps, stop stirring with the stick blender. Immediately, and slowly, begin hand stirring to disperse any pockets of fragrance or essential oils or any other additives that may have caused the lumping. If the entire mixture appears to be solidifying, immediately pour or scoop the mixture into the soap mold (see troubleshooting for seizing on page 136).

Signs of Trouble in Finished Soap

For safety reasons, it is **always important to inspect your soap** when you release it from the mold, and again when you cut the soap into individual bars. Next we'll discuss problems that may appear in finished soap.

Problem: Lye Pockets

Lye pockets are small or large holes in finished soap that hold liquid or appear to be seeping liquid, which is often unmixed lye solution.

How to Avoid

Soap that contains large or small holes that appears to seep or hold liquids must be discarded. The oils and lye have separated, creating lye pockets.

Lye pockets normally occur when the soap mixture is not properly blended before it is poured into the mold. Occasionally, an entire batch, log or loaf of soap contains large tunnels of lye.

Use extreme caution. Wear gloves, long-sleeved clothing and eye protection. Immediately discard the entire batch of soap!

Problem: Hard, Brittle, Crumbly and White

Finished soap that is hard, brittle, crumbly or white.

How to Avoid

Hard and brittle soap normally indicates that too much lye was used in the formula. Check your measurements for accuracy. Soap made with too much lye usually isn't mild enough for use on the skin. Discard the soap.

Dry, brittle soap can also result from a formula that contains too high of a percentage of hard oils such as tallow or cocoa butter. Check your formula to see if this might have been the issue and adjust as necessary.

Problem: Fragrance Too Light

This problem occurs when the fragrance (scent) is too light in finished soap.

How to Avoid

Check the ratios and measurements of the fragrance and/or essential oils that you used in the formula. You may have used too little. Remember to use enough to scent the soap, but do not exceed the recommended usage guidelines determined by the fragrance oil supplier or manufacturer. See Chapter 8 for recommended essential oil usage.

Some essential oils, especially those in the citrus family, and some fragrance oils, are not suitable for cold process alkaline conditions and will evaporate quickly. There are some solutions, though. For instance, you can use litsea cubeba essential oil to anchor the scent of lemon essential oil so that the scent will last longer in the finished soap.

Adding essential or fragrance oils to a soap mixture that is too hot may cause them to evaporate during the soap making process. Always blend at the correct temperature.

Problem: Grainy or "Riced"
This is when finished soap that appears grainy or looks like it has pieces of rice throughout.

How to Avoid
Soap that is grainy or appears to be riced is usually an aesthetic issue. The soap can likely still be used, but its appearance may not make it suitable for sale.

Graininess in soap can also be caused by soap that is mixed at too low of a temperature.

Graininess in soap can also be caused by a soap formula that was not mixed briskly and consistently before it was poured into the mold.

See the troubleshooting section for rings on page 142 when portions of the finished soap are soft or grainy.

Graininess is common when goat milk with a very high fat content is used in a formula. Try using more water in the formula and less milk.

Problem: Soft or Spongy
This problem is noticeable at the end of a standard (approximately 4 week) cure time, and the finished soap is still very soft or spongy.

How to Avoid
Soft or spongy soap normally reflects a formula that did not include enough lye or a formula in which a high percentage of soft oils are used. Check your measurements and your formula.

Continue to allow the soap to cure. The soap may harden over an extended (greater than 4-6 week) period of time. If the soap remains soft or spongy, it can safely be used, however, it may not be suitable for retail sale.

Certain ingredients tend to produce a softer soap, one that takes longer to harden or cure, such as castor oil, some citrus oils and milk. Allow an additional two weeks of curing time for soaps produced with these ingredients.

See the troubleshooting section for rings on page 142 when portions of the finished soap are soft.

Problem: Oil on Top

Oil on top of finished soap.

How to Avoid

A very light film of oil, or droplets on the top of a newly made batch of soap does not necessarily indicate a problem. If the oil is very thin it will likely absorb into the soap during the curing process.

A heavy film of oil on top of the soap can be caused by any of the following: not enough mixing of the batch prior to pouring, ingredient proportions that were incorrect, or a drop in temperature after the soap was poured into the mold.

Check the soap formula and precisely measure the ingredients. For non-milk soap, insulate the soap as soon as possible after pouring it into the mold to ensure changes in room temperature do not affect the soap. For milk soap, insulate as soon as possible if the room temperature is cool or drafty.

Allow the soap to cure for 4-6 weeks. If the soap is mild, meaning there are no holes or seepage of lye affecting other areas of the soap, or hard white spots, soap with a very light oily film on top can be safely used, but may not be aesthetically suitable to sell.

Problem: Cracks

Cracks on the top of finished soap.

How to Avoid

Cracks on the top of soap may be caused by too much lye in the formula.

Cracks can also indicate too much stirring of the soap mixture, causing it to set too quickly.

Formulas with higher proportions of some butters and oils such as castor oil and cocoa butter are more prone to cracking.

Unless the soap also contains white pockets (pockets of lye) or if it is too hard or brittle, soap with small cracks is safe for use.

Problem: Brown/Orange Spots

Brown or orange spots appearing in finished soap.

How to Avoid

Brown or orange spots that appear in the soap are an indication of oxidation of excess oils in the soap. This means the oils have gone rancid. Discard the soap.

Excess heat in the curing area can promote oxidation.

Curing areas are optimal at room temperature with average to low humidity. Using a dehumidifier in the curing area with no excess heat helps to prevent brown/orange spots.

Check the soap formula. Ensure the lye, water and oil proportions are accurate.

Orange spots in finished soap can also be small particles of lye that did not dissolve; this is common when goat milk is used as the liquid in a soap formula. Always pour the milk/lye solution through a sieve when adding to the oils to ensure hard particles of un-dissolved lye are not added to the soap mixture. **Soap containing un-dissolved lye must be discarded.**

Problem: White Film on Top

White film on top of finished soap.

How to Avoid

Soda ash is a thin white film (only on the top) which can be caused by not covering the newly poured batch of soap with plastic wrap, allowing too much air to reach the soap.

A thin white film can also indicate that the soap was made with water that was too hard. Always use distilled water.
The thin white film is not dangerous, it can be washed or trimmed off, or used as is.

See the troubleshooting section for Hard, Brittle, Crumbly and White on page 138 if the body of the finished soap contains white streaks or pockets.

A formula containing milk often leaves a thin white film on the top of the finished soap. The film is more obvious when the finished soap is darker in color.

Problem: Soap Turned to Liquid in the Mold or There is Liquid in the Bottom of Mold

Description
Finished soap that has turned to liquid in the mold, or there is liquid in the bottom of the mold.

How to Avoid
The soap mixture reached a false trace and was not properly mixed prior to pouring.

The soap is caustic and must be discarded.

Use caution; wear gloves, long sleeves and eye protection while discarding the soap. Discard the soap mixture using the same precautions as you would for the disposal of lye, see page 18.

Problem: Rings

Description
Finished soap with the appearance of rings or inner layers.

How to Avoid
Insulate soap in the mold according to instructions and pay close attention to the ambient room temperature. Soap that is poured into the mold in a room much cooler than room temperature, or one that is subject to drafts may not completely go through the chemical phases that are needed while in the mold.

The soap can be used unless the soap within the rings is too soft or crumbly.

Cautions
Goat milk contains natural sugars that speed up the saponification process. Use caution when adding ingredients to a formula that are high in sugar content, such as honey or wine. Always add high-sugar content ingredients when the soap has reached trace, and be prepared for any potential volcano effects (see the Volcano Effect on page 135 for more information.)

RESOURCE DIRECTORY

There are a number of resources for you to tap into as you are developing and growing your soap making skills. Of course, we're going to recommend our services first and foremost! Mary is an expert in using goat milk in formulations from soaps to lotions and beyond. Alyssa is an expert in providing bath and body business-specific training, coaching and resources.

Finally, the Indie Business Network (IBN) is a top-notch industry resource. IBN will help you connect with other soap makers around the world, with great opportunities to keep you informed of new trends in the marketplace, get your questions answered and learn about developments or changes in industry regulations.

Mary Humphrey
www.anniesgoathill.com
anniesgoathill@gmail.com

Alyssa Middleton
Bath and Body Academy
www.bathandbodyacademy.com
Alyssa@bathandbodyacademy.com

Indie Business Network
(704) 291-7280
www.indiebusinessnetwork.com

PURCHASING INGREDIENTS, SUPPLIES AND PACKAGING

Below are reputable companies we recommend when buying ingredients and supplies. Although there are many supply companies out there, only stores we have had a positive experience with are listed. Most of these companies offer products in a variety of categories, but we have only listed each company under its primary category here.

Note that not all of these suppliers have "drop-in" or local pickup capabilities, so be sure to contact them prior to stopping into their offices.

General Soap Making Supplies

Brambleberry Soap Making Supplies
2138 Humboldt Street
Bellingham, WA 98225
(360) 734-8278
www.brambleberry.com

Cibaria International
1203 Hall Avenue
Riverside, CA 92509
(951) 823-8490
www.cibariasoapsupply.com

Elements Bath and Body Supply
Crestwood, KY 40014
(502) 690-2520
www.elementsbathandbody.com

Essential Wholesale
2211 NW Nicolai St
Portland, OR 97210
(503) 722-7557
(866) 252-9639
www.essentialwholesale.com

From Nature With Love
Natural Sourcing, LLC
341 Christian Street
Oxford, CT 06478
(800) 520-2060
www.fromnaturewithlove.com

Lotioncrafter
532 Point Lawrence Road
Olga, WA 98279
(866) 490-9587
www.lotioncrafter.com

Majestic Mountain Sage
2490 South 1350 West
Nibley, UT 84321
(435) 755-0863
www.thesage.com

Nature's Garden
42109 State Route 18
Wellington, OH 44090
(440) 647-0100
(866) 647-2368
www.naturesgardencandles.com

Organic Creations
2420 NW Campus Drive, Suite E
Estacada, OR 97023
(503) 630-3237
www.organic-creations.com

Soapalooza!
700 E Main St #34
Richmond, VA 23218
(804) 447-5400
www.soapalooza.com

The Herbarie
630 Turner Road
Prosperity, SC 29127
(803) 364-9979
www.theherbarie.com

The Original Soap Dish
PO Box 263
South Whitley, IN 46787
(260) 723-4039
www.thesoapdish.com

Wholesale Supplies Plus
10035 Broadview Road
Broadview Heights, OH 44147
(800) 359-0944
www.wholesalesuppliesplus.com

Equipment

For Craft's Sake
28327 180th Street
Starbuck, MN 56381
(320) 239-3171
www.forcraftssake.com

Soap Equipment (a division of Willow Way LLC)
12873 W E Oler
Hagerstown, IN 47346
(765) 886-4640
www.soapequipment.com

Herbs

Glenbrook Farms
1538 Shiloh Road
Campbellsville, KY 42718
(888) 716-7627
www.glenbrookfarm.com

Mountain Rose Herbs
PO Box 50220
Eugene, OR 97405
(541) 741-7307
(800) 879-3337
www.mountainroseherbs.com

San Francisco Herb Company
250 14th Street
San Francisco, CA 94103
(800) 227-4530
www.sfherb.com

Labels

Labels By The Sheet / Creative Label Concepts
1328 East Empire Street
Suites A & B
Bloomington, IL 61701
(309) 665-0130
www.labelsbythesheet.com

Lightning Labels
2369 S Trenton Way, Unit C
Denver, CO 80231
(888) 907-3004
(303) 695-0398
www.lighninglabels.com

Online Labels
975 Bennett Drive
Longwood, FL 32750
(888) 575-2235
www.onlinelabels.com

Fragrance / Essential Oils

Bulk Apothecary / Nature's Oil Products
1800 Miller Parkway
Streetsboro, OH 44241
(888) 968-7220
www.bulkapothecary.com

Camden Grey Essential Oils Inc.
3579 NW 82nd Avenue
Doral, FL 33122
(305) 500-9630
www.camdengrey.com

New Directions Aromatics
60 Industrial Parkway, Suite 325
Cheektowaga, NY 14227
(800) 246-7817
www.newdirectionsaromatics.com

The Lebermuth Company
14000 McKinley Highway
Mishawaka, IN 46545
(800) 648-1123
www.lebermuth.com

Oils and Butters
*at the time of printing they sell sustainable palm oil

Ciranda Inc*
221 Vine Street
Hudson, WI 54016
(715) 386-1737
www.ciranda.com

Jedwards International
39 Broad Street
Quincy, MA 02169
(617) 472-9300
www.bulknaturaloils.com

Shea Butter Hut
PO Box 304
Harrison, TN 37341
(866) 517-6407
www.sheabutterhut.com

Soapers Choice*
30 E. Oakton Street
Des Plaines, IL 60018
(800) 322-6457, ext. 8930
www.soaperschoice.com

Packaging

McKenzie Crest, Inc / Custom Kraft Box
2095 Laura Street
Springfield, OR 97477
(877) 300-2405
www.mckenziecrest.com

Nashville Wraps
242 Molly Walton Drive
Hendersonville, TN 37075
(800) 547-9727
www.nashvillewraps.com

The Box Co-op
938 S Andreasen Dr, St K
Escondido, CA 92029
(800) 555-1778
www.boxcoop.com

Shipping Supplies

Cheep Cheep Boxes
PO Box 236
Middletown, OH 45042
(513) 217-5560
(877) 269-3745
www.cheepcheepboxes.com

Uline
12575 Uline Drive
Pleasant Prairie, WI 53158
(800) 295-5510
www.uline.com

Soap Molds

Kelsei's Creations
PO Box 37
Westbrook, TX 79565
(806) 570-9527
www.kelseiscreations.com

Milky Way Molds
4207 SE Woodstock
Portland, OR 97206
(800) 588-7930
www.milkywaymolds.com

Soap Hutch
4106A Sequoia Trail West
Georgetown, TX 78628
(510) 868-2862
www.soaphutch.com

Soap Making Resource
355 E Liberty St. Suite C
Lancaster, PA 17602
(717) 875-8670
www.soap-making-resource.com

Sodium Hydroxide (Lye)

AAA Chemicals, Inc.
226 Texas City Wye
LaMarque, TX 77568
(409) 908-0070
www.aaa-chemicals.com

Boyer Corporation
PO Box 10
LaGrange, IL 60525
(800) 323-3040
www.boyercorporation.com

Certified Lye / Acute Soap Enterprises LLC
PO Box 133
Spring Valley, CA 91976
(619) 548-2378
www.certified-lye.com

Essential Depot
2029 US Hwy 27 South
Sebring, FL 33870
(866) 840-2495
www.essentialdepot.com

The Chemistry Store
1133 Walter Price Street
Cayce, SC 29033
(800) 224-1430
www.chemistrystore.com

GLOSSARY

A

Abrasives: Also called an exfoliant. Gritty or rough ingredients that are added to soap to help scrub away dirt or dead outer skin cells.

Absolute: A concentrated, highly aromatic mixture extracted from plants via alcohol and vacuum distillation. Absolutes are an alcohol soluble aromatic base.

Acid: A substance with a pH less than 7.

Additives: Any ingredient other than water, lye, oils or butters that is added to soap. Examples include colorants, herbs, fragrance or essential oils, and antioxidants.

Alkali: Also called a base. A substance with a pH greater than 7. An alkali can be used to neutralize an acid. Sodium hydroxide (lye) is an alkali.

Allergen: A substance that can cause an allergic reaction. Using nut oils (peanut, hazelnut, macadamia, etc) or gluten-containing oils such as wheat germ in soap can cause a person with allergies to these substances to have an allergic reaction.

Antibacterial: A substance that can effectively destroy bacteria.

Antioxidant: Prevents or slows oxidation. In soaping, these substances help block the process of oxygen reacting with oils and causing them to go rancid. Antioxidant properties in soap help prolong the life of the oils in your soap. Examples of antioxidants include vitamin E and rosemary oleoresin extract. Some oils have naturally high levels of vitamin E, including high oleic sunflower or wheat germ oil, and are added to formulas to help prolong the lives of other oils in the formula. Antioxidants are <u>not</u> the same as preservatives.

Antiseptic: A substance that has the ability to fight infection.

Aromatherapy: The use of essential oils to alter and enhance general health and well-being.

Aromatic: Having a strong fragrance or odor.

Astringent: A substance used to tighten skin and remove excess oil from skin.

B

Base: The alkali used in soap making, such as sodium hydroxide (lye).

Base Oils: Also known as fixed oils; these are the main oils that make up the soap formula, such as coconut, palm and olive oils.

Botanical: A substance obtained from a plant's parts.

Botanical Name: Also known as the International Nomenclature of Cosmetics Ingredients (INCI) name. The Latin name assigned to distinguish one species from another, the scientific name composed of the genus followed by the species.

C

Carrier Oil: A vegetable or nut base oil used to dilute essential oils prior to applying to the skin.

Castile: A region in Spain known for producing olive oil based soaps in the 13th century. Today, a soap made with 100% olive oil is referred to as a Castile soap. Some soap makers call a soap with *mostly* olive oil Castile.

Caustic: A corrosive substance that burns through a chemical action. Caustic can refer to an acid or a base but is typically used to describe the action of an alkaline base. Sodium hydroxide (lye) is caustic.

Caustic Potash: Also known as potassium hydroxide. This is the alkali (base) used in liquid soap making.

Caustic Soda: Also known as sodium hydroxide (lye). This is the alkali (base) used in bar soap making.

Cold Pressed: A method for extracting oils from raw materials. Oil is extracted through mechanical pressure at low temperatures, typically less than 125°F. Cold pressing preserves the benefits and properties of the oils.

Cold Process: Also known as CP. A method of soap making without utilizing any external heat source other than to melt the hard oils.

Cosmetic: A product applied to the human body for cleansing, beautifying, promoting attractiveness, or altering ones' appearance. Products deemed cosmetics are regulated in the United States by the Food and Drug Administration.

Cosmetic Grade: A designation by the United States government that the product has been approved for use directly on the skin.

Crock Pot Hot Process: Also called CPHP, a method of soap making using the heat from an electric crock pot during the soap making process.

Cruelty Free: Not tested on animals.

Cure: Also known as the aging process of soap. This is the time period between making the soap and using the soap. Soap should cure for at least 4-6 weeks before it is used. During this time, the soap becomes mild and excess water evaporates, making the bar harden and last longer.

D

D&C: An acronym that stands for Drugs & Cosmetics. The term is used to designate the United States Government's approved use in drugs (external use only) and cosmetics, such as D&C Red#7.

Decoction: An extract of brewed hard plant material such as bark or root. Extracted by boiling the plant material to obtain various properties.

Deodorize: To remove scent. Some oils are refined and deodorized before selling to remove the scent so that they do not bring an additional odor to the finished product in which the oil is used.

Detergent: A surfactant that acts similarly to soap in terms of cleansing, but is not created by the saponification of fats and oils. A common detergent used in commercially made soap is sodium laurel sulfate.

Dreaded Orange Spots: Small yellow-orange spots that appear on the surface of cold process soap; primarily thought to be a result of unsaponified oils going rancid. Also called DOS. DOS is more prevalent in highly superfatted soaps.

Discounted Water Cold Process: A cold process method of soap making using a lower percentage of water in the formula for a stronger lye solution. Also called DWCP.

E

Emollient: A substance used to soften or soothe skin. Examples include shea or cocoa butter, and glycerin.

Essential Oil: A highly concentrated, volatile oil extracted from aromatic plants, most commonly through pressing or steam distillation. Also called EO.

Exfoliant: Also known as an abrasive. Gritty or rough ingredients added to soap to help scrub away dirt or dead outer skin cells.

Exothermic: A chemical reaction that releases heat. Soap is made as the product of an exothermic reaction between lye and fat (oils).

Expeller Pressed: The mechanical method for extracting oils from raw materials. Oil is extracted from a base by mechanically crushing and pressing the material at temperatures of less than 210°F.

Extract: A substance, extracted from a plant through distillation, pressure or solvents, containing its essence in concentrated form.

F
Fatty Acids: Compounds of carbon, oxygen and hydrogen found in fats and oils. They can be saturated or unsaturated, and in soap, fatty acids are what give soap their bubbly lather, hardness, cleansing and conditioning characteristics.

FD&C: An acronym that stands for Food, Drugs & Cosmetics. The term is used to designate the United States Government's approved use in food, drugs (external use only) and cosmetics.

Fixed Oils: Also known as base oils. These are the main oils that make up the soap formula, such as coconut, palm and olive oils.

Flash Point: The lowest temperature at which the vapors of a liquid can ignite. Some fixed oils and essential oils have low flash points, so soap makers must be aware of this during the soap making process, as items with low flash points can burst into flames when heated.

French Milled Soap: Also known as hand-milled. Pre-made soap is grated, mixed with liquids, gently heated and pressed into molds.

Formula: A listing of ingredients in fixed proportions, typically expressed in percentages.

Fragrance Oil: Synthetically scented oil formulated to mimic natural fragrances. Used when a particular scent cannot be created naturally, such as by essential oils. Also called FO.

G

Gel: Also known as gel phase or gel stage. An early phase of the saponification process when the temperature of the soap batter increases after being poured into the mold. The soap temporarily becomes a translucent gel and slowly returns to a solid, cooler mass. Not all soap batches go through a gel phase. Some soap makers prefer their soaps to gel and others do not. It is a matter of personal preference.

Glycerin: A thick, sticky, clear substance naturally created during the process of saponification. Glycerin has emollient and humectant properties. Handmade cold process and hot process soaps retain the glycerin created in the soap making process. Commercial 'soaps' often remove the glycerin from their final product.

H

Handmade Soap: Soap made by combining base oil(s) with an alkali using traditional methods including hot and cold processing.

Hand Milled: Also known as French milled. Pre-made soap is grated, mixed with liquids, gently heated and pressed into molds.

Herb: An aromatic plant that does not produce woody tissue, and usually dies back at the end of the growing season.

Hot Process: Also known as HP. A method of soap making that uses heat to speed up the saponification process.

Humectant: A substance that attracts and retains moisture, such as glycerin.

Hydrogenated Oil: Unsaturated oils with added hydrogen to create a solid oil that is more resistant to spoiling.

Hydrogenation: A chemical process of converting a vegetable oil from a liquid into a solid using hydrogen.

Hydrosol: Also known as floral water. When an essential oil is steam distilled from plant material the oil is collected as an essential oil. The remaining water is collected as a hydrosol. Hydrosols are not highly concentrated, so they are not suitable for cold process soap formulations. They are used for natural scent blends, lotions and cosmetics, and are sprayed directly on the skin as a light moisturizer.

Hygroscopic: The tendency of a material to absorb and retain moisture from the air. Sodium hydroxide (lye) has hygroscopic properties.

Hypoallergenic: A substance unlikely to cause an allergic reaction.

I

Industrial Nomenclature of Cosmetic Ingredients (INCI): A system of names for ingredients that must be used when labeling soaps and cosmetics. Each country has different regulations regarding when the INCI name must be included on product labels.

Industrial Grade: A designation by the United States government that refers to the intended use of a product. Industrial grade products are not intended for use directly on the skin. **Do not use industrial grade ingredients in soap or cosmetic making**; use cosmetic or food grade ingredients instead.

Infusion: A liquid extract made by steeping botanical matter in oil or water to extract various properties of the plant material.

Insoluble: A substance that is incapable of being dissolved in a liquid such as water or alcohol.

L

Litmus paper: A strip of paper containing a mixture of water-soluble dyes used to indicate the pH level of a substance. Blue litmus paper turns red under acidic conditions and red litmus paper turns blue under alkaline conditions. Neutral litmus paper is purple. Litmus paper simply determines whether a solution is acidic or alkaline, it does not measure the strength of the acid or base.

Lye: Also known as sodium hydroxide or caustic soda. This is the alkali (base) used in bar soap making.

M

Manufacturer's Grade: A designation by the United States government that the product has been approved for use in the manufacturing of another product. These products have not been approved for direct application on the skin, but they can be used when making soap or candles. Some fragrance oils come in manufacturer's grades.

Melt and Pour Soap: A pre-made soap base designed to melt, mix with certain additives and pour into molds. The soap is ready to be used once it hardens.

Melting Point: The temperature at which a solid becomes a liquid.

Material Safety Data Sheet or Safety Data Sheet: A report provided by the manufacturer or distributor to define the health, safety and fire risks associated with a substance and outlines how to handle and work with the substance in a safe manner. Also known as MSDS or SDS.

Mucilaginous: A moist and/or sticky substance, with a mucus type consistency.

N

NaOH: The molecular formula for sodium hydroxide, also known as lye or caustic soda.

O

Organic: A substance that at one time was alive and has not had chemicals or synthetic materials introduced to it.

Oxidation: A chemical reaction with oxygen. In soap making, oxidation of oils can cause the oil to go rancid. Using antioxidants in the soap formula may inhibit oxidation and help prevent Dreaded Orange Spots in the soap.

P

pH: A measurement of the acidity or alkalinity of a substance. The scale ranges from 0 (highly acidic) to 14 (highly alkaline or highly basic). A pH value of 7 is neutral, a pH less than 7 is acidic and a pH of more than 7 is alkaline, also called basic. Sodium hydroxide, or lye has a pH of 14. Water has a pH of 7. Most cured soaps have a pH range of 8-10.

pH Test Strip: A strip of special paper used to determine the approximate pH of a substance.

Photosensitizer: A substance that can cause skin to be more prone to sunburn when exposed to sunlight.

Phototoxic: Creating sun sensitivity. Some essential oils contain constituents that intensely absorb sunlight, and using or leaving on products that contain these essential oils may cause skin to react with sun exposure.

Potassium Hydroxide: Also known as caustic potash, this is the alkali (base) used in liquid soap making.

Preservative: A substance that inhibits bacterial or mold growth.

R
Rancidity: Having an unpleasant, stale smell, as a result of decomposition or spoilage making it unfit or unsafe for use.

Rebatching: A soap making process where shreds of cold process soap and liquid are gently heated, then color and/or fragrance are added to create a new bar of soap.

Refined: The process of removing impurities from the natural base.

Rendering: The process of heating lard or tallow to a liquid state to remove solids or impurities.

Ricing: An effect that appears as though the finished soap has pieces of rice throughout. Can be caused by certain fragrance oils or by not blending the soap mixture enough before pouring into the mold. Ricing does not affect the performance of the soap, just the appearance.

Room Temperature Cold Process: A cold process soap making method that calls for oils to be at room temperature when the lye solution is added. Also known as RTCP.

S
Saponification Value (SAP): The amount of milligrams of sodium hydroxide required to saponify 1 gram of fat (oil).

Saponification: The chemical reaction between a base (fat or oil) and an alkali (sodium hydroxide/lye) to produce a salt (soap) and a free alcohol (glycerin).

Sebum: The fatty substance secreted by the sebaceous glands of the skin. Sebum is the skin's natural oil.

Seizing: The unexpected solidifying of soap batter during processing, making it unable to be mixed or poured. Seizing results from using some fragrance or essential oils, waxes or the temperature of the oils in the soap batter.

Soap: A simple cleansing agent; the sodium salt resulting from the combination of oils and fats with an alkali.

Soda Ash: A harmless but unsightly powdery white residue that can form on the surface of soap. It may result from excess oxygen exposure during the cooling and curing process. Soap with soda ash may be used as is, but the ash can be cut off the soap for a more visually appealing bar.

Sodium Hydroxide: Also known as NaOH, lye or caustic soda, this is the alkali (base) used in bar soap making.

Soluble: A substance that is capable of being dissolved or liquefied.

Solvent Extraction: A method for extracting oils from raw materials. Oil is separated from the base using a liquid solvent. The oil is then distilled and the solvent evaporates, leaving only the oil.

Steam Distillation: The steam and pressure method used to extract essential oils from plant materials.

Superfatting: The addition of extra oils or butters that remain unsaponified within the finished soap. These excess oils and butters contribute to the moisturizing properties of the soap.

Surfactant: A substance that reduces the surface tension of the liquid in which it is dissolved. A surfactant assists in releasing dirt and oils from surfaces when water is added.

Sweating: The appearance of sweat-looking beads on finished bars of soap. This can be caused by using Dead Sea salt in salt bar formulas. Sweating does not affect the performance of the soap, just the appearance.

Synthetic: A substance that is artificially produced, not of natural origin.

T
Tocopherol: Any of the four forms (alpha-, beta-, delta- or gamma-) of vitamin E, an antioxidant added to soaps as an emollient and antioxidant. Alpha-tocopherol has greatest amount of vitamin E.

Trace: A point in soap making where the mixture reaches a noticeable thickness. Trace is often recognized when the soap is drizzled upon itself and leaves a trail before disappearing back into the mixture.

U

Unrefined: The natural, unaltered base, such as the oil obtained from the first pressing.

Unsaponifiables: Components that do not react with sodium hydroxide during saponification and remain in their original state. These components contribute moisturizing or other skin nourishing properties to the finished soap.

V

Vegan: not containing any animal oils such as lard or tallow, or any ingredients produced by animals, such as beeswax, honey or silk.

Vegetarian: Not containing any animal-derived ingredients, such as lard or tallow.

Vegetable Shortening: A solid fat made by hydrogenating vegetable oils.

Viscosity: A measurement of the resistance of a substance to flow. It is commonly referred to as thickness or resistance to pouring.

Volatile Oils: Oils that evaporate or vaporize easily. Essential oils are highly volatile.

Volcano Effect: An unexpected and potentially dangerous occurrence where the soap mixture overheats and boils over either out of the soap pot or mold. Can be caused by certain ingredients that tend to overheat, including honey and milk.

W

Water Discount: The process of using less than 100 percent of the water recommended by a lye calculator for your soap formula. Soap makers use a water discount to shorten the drying process and/or increase trace.

Water Soluble: A substance that is dissolvable in water.

APPENDIX 1
ONLINE LYE CALCULATORS

Online lye calculators can help you quickly and accurately design and calculate unique soap formulas. Each of the online calculators listed below are widely used in the soap making industry.

Brambleberry
http://www.brambleberry.com/pages/Lye-Calculator.aspx
(also available as a (paid) app for iPhone, iPad and iTouch)

Handmade Soap Makers Guild
http://www.soapguild.org/soap makers/resources/lye-calc.php

Majestic Mountain Sage
https://www.thesage.com/calcs/lyecalc2.php

SoapCalc
http://www.soapcalc.net/calc/soapcalcwp.asp

Summer Bee Meadow
https://summerbeemeadow.com/content/lye-calculator-and-recipe-resizer
(also has a feature to resize your formula for different sized molds)

APPENDIX 2
WEIGHT AND MEASUREMENT CONVERSIONS

We teach soap making formulas by the weight. Occasionally, a recipe is found that requires measurement conversions.

MEASUREMENT CONVERSIONS BY VOLUME			
.5 fl ounces	1 Tbl	15 mL	1/16 cup
1 fl ounce	2 Tbl	29.57 mL	1/8 cup
8 fl ounces	16 Tbl	236.56 mL	1 cup
16 fl ounces	32 Tbl	473.12 mL	2 cup
32 fl ounces	64 Tbl	946.24 mL	4 cups
64 fl ounces	½ gallon	1892.48 mL	8 cups
128 fl ounces	1 gallon	3784.96 mL	16 cups

To convert US measurements into metric measurements, follow these conversion guidelines:

Ounce (oz) x 28.3 = Gram (g)

Quart (qt) x 0.9 = Litre (l)

Gallon (gal) x 0.004 = Cubic metre (m3)

MEASUREMENT CONVERSIONS BY WEIGHT				
1 ounce		0.625 lb	0.028 kg	28.35 g
1 pound (lb)	16 oz		0.453 kg	453.59 g
1 kilogram (kg)	35.27 oz	2.2046 lbs		1000 g
1 gram (g)	0.35 oz	.002204 lbs	0.001 kg	

APPENDIX 3
EDITING TEAM

We are indebted to our editing team who spent hours reviewing and helping us revise different iterations of this manuscript.

Elin Criswell, author of *Creative Soap Making*
www.TheCountrySoaper.com
www.LoneStarSoapAndToiletries.com
Facebook.com/TheCountrySoaper

Terri Lang Patterson, owner of Body Systems
www.body-systems.net

Alana Rivera, Soap Maven + CEO Etta+Billie
www.ettaandbillie.com
Facebook.com/EttaandBillie
Twitter.com/alanarivera
Twitter.com/ettaandbillie

Anne Marie Rowe
Caregiver Empowerment Partner at Rowe Together
www.rowetogether.com
Facebook.com/RoweTogether

Robin Schmidt, owner of Dragonfly Soap
www.drangonflyhandmadesoap.com
Facebook.com/drgnflysoap

Maia Singletary, owner of Astrida Naturals
www.astridanaturals.com
Facebook.com/AstridaNaturals

Rachel Turner, owner of Music City Suds
www.MusicCitySuds.com
Facebook.com/MusicCitySuds

Ann McIntire Wooledge, RN, CCAP, owner of Wingsets
www.Wingsets.com
Facebook.com/WingsetsAromatherapy
Twitter.com/wingsets

INDEX

ABOUT THE AUTHORS

Your trusted guides in this book are Mary Humphrey and Alyssa Middleton. We are both experienced at handcrafting personal care products and running successful small businesses. We have included our experiences, tips and tricks in this book to save you time and energy through your soaping adventures.

Mary Humphrey is the owner of Annie's Goat Hill. She has been handcrafting soap for 10 years, and has also lovingly raised a herd of dairy goats for many of those years, which led her to include the rich milk produced on her farm in her soaps. Mary's interests and studies include aromatherapy – the study of the value and health benefits of plant-based materials. Mary also authors under her business name His Pasture Press. She writes posts (and upcoming books) based on the principle of: Share, Encourage, and Grow.

Mary's website: www.AnniesGoatHill.com

Alyssa Middleton has been making soap and body care products for 15 years and in 2007 bought Vintage Body Spa . In 2011, she opened the Bath and Body Academy to teach and serve current and aspiring body care business owners in building their beauty empires.

Alyssa's websites:
www.bathandbodyacademy.com
www.vintagebodyspa.com

www.ingramcontent.com/pod-product-compliance
Lightning Source LLC
LaVergne TN
LVHW081353060426
835510LV00013B/1797